An Unpleasant Predicament

A Darkly Comic Tale of Pride, Chaos, and Social Satire

A Modern Translation

Adapted for the Contemporary Reader

Fyodor Dostoevsky

Table of Contents

Preface - Message to the Reader

Rebuilding the Greatest Library in Human History

Thousands of years ago, the Library of Alexandria was the heart of global knowledge — a sanctuary where the wisdom of every known civilization was gathered and shared freely.

And then, it was lost.

Now, we're rebuilding it — and you are invited to join us.

At the Library of Alexandria, we've set out to make every book available to *every person on Earth* — not just in print, but in every language, every format, and for every reader.

Here's how we do it:

- **Deluxe Print Editions at True Printing Cost** - Order any book as a high-quality paperback, elegant hardcover, or stunning boxset — and only pay what it costs to print. No markups. No middlemen.
- **Unlimited Access to the Greatest Works** - Enjoy thousands of timeless classics — from Plato to Shakespeare to Tolstoy — in beautiful, modern eBook and audiobook editions. Read and listen without limits — for every reader, everywhere.
- **Modern Translations for Every Language & Dialect** - We're reimagining the classics in clear, accessible language — and translating them into every dialect imaginable. Everyone deserves to understand humanity's greatest ideas.

When you visit **LibraryofAlexandria.com**, you're not just accessing books — you're joining a global movement to restore, preserve, and share the wisdom of civilization.

Join us today at LibraryofAlexandria.com

Together, we'll ensure the light of human wisdom never fades again.

With gratitude,
The Modern Library of Alexandria Team

Visit:

www.libraryofalexandria.com

Or scan the code below:

Introduction

Satire, Status, and the Absurdity of the Bureaucratic Mind

An Unpleasant Predicament (sometimes translated as A Nasty Anecdote) is one of Fyodor Dostoevsky's most overlooked yet brilliantly executed short works. Written in 1862, it was composed during a significant period in Dostoevsky's life when he was reestablishing himself as a leading literary figure in Russia following years of exile and imprisonment. Though it lacks the overtly tragic depth of his major novels, this satirical gem offers razor-sharp insight into the psychology of social performance, status anxiety, and the absurdity of bureaucratic pride. With its darkly comic tone, the story functions as both a hilarious farce and a deeply revealing psychological study.

At the center of the story is Ivan Ilyich Pralinsky, a high-ranking civil servant who, inspired by lofty ideals of human equality and benevolence, decides to attend the wedding of a lowly subordinate—completely uninvited. What begins as a supposedly noble and spontaneous gesture quickly devolves into a disastrous evening of social blunders, drunken confusion, and self-inflicted humiliation. Pralinsky's internal justification for his actions—his desire to demonstrate the unity of all classes—is systematically dismantled by his own ego, obliviousness, and the jarring reality of class division in 19th-century Russian society.

Despite its brevity, An Unpleasant Predicament operates on multiple levels. It is a work of biting political satire, a psychological character sketch, and a critique of idealistic liberal humanism disconnected from real-life human dignity. The story invites us to laugh at Pralinsky's ridiculousness, but it also forces us to reflect on how often our own attempts at virtue are compromised by ego, pride, and social blindness.

This introduction will examine the thematic significance, psychological depth, and historical context of An Unpleasant Predicament, and explain why this short story deserves far more recognition than it typically receives. While comedic in tone, it stands shoulder-to-shoulder with Dostoevsky's more somber masterpieces in its exploration of moral ambiguity and human contradiction.

The Fallibility of Good Intentions

Ivan Ilyich Pralinsky is a bureaucrat in the highest sense of the word. He is self-important, rule-bound, and obsessed with appearances—yet at the same time, he

4

fancies himself a progressive humanitarian. Early in the story, he delivers a heartfelt speech about the need for mutual respect between social classes, declaring that kindness and dignity can unite all people regardless of rank. On the surface, this seems noble, even enlightened. But Dostoevsky, never content with easy answers, quickly begins to dismantle this idealism.

When Pralinsky learns that one of his underlings, Pseldonymov, is getting married, he decides—on a sudden emotional impulse—that he must personally attend the wedding to show solidarity with the lower classes. He imagines his unexpected appearance will be taken as a symbol of his generosity and moral greatness. In his mind, the entire event becomes a theatrical performance with himself at center stage, playing the role of the magnanimous benefactor.

The irony is that Pralinsky, for all his grand ideals, has no understanding of the people he is trying to uplift. He barges into the wedding like an elephant into a porcelain shop, oblivious to the discomfort his presence causes. The family is horrified, the bride is terrified, and the groom is mortified. Instead of bridging the class divide, Pralinsky's visit exacerbates it, exposing the gulf between his well-meaning fantasies and the actual lived experiences of those beneath him in status.

Dostoevsky's portrayal of Pralinsky is brutal and hilarious in equal measure. The story becomes an escalating series of cringe-inducing moments: Pralinsky tries to make a toast and stumbles; he lectures the guests on equality while clearly expecting deference; he forces affection where none is welcome. The climax comes when he, completely drunk, falls asleep in the bridal chamber—an act of mortifying impropriety that underscores how thoroughly he has misunderstood his place and misjudged the nature of his gesture.

Yet Dostoevsky refuses to reduce Pralinsky to a caricature. The story is a comedy, yes, but it is tinged with melancholy. Pralinsky genuinely wants to do good. He is not malicious—only blind. His humiliation is tragic because it stems from a sincere, if misguided, desire to be a better man. Dostoevsky thus invites the reader to both laugh at and sympathize with him, to recognize in his blundering performance something universal: the human tendency to mistake ego for virtue, and good intentions for wisdom.

An Unpleasant Predicament is, in this way, a story about the limits of liberal idealism unmoored from lived experience. Pralinsky's belief in social unity is not grounded in actual solidarity or humility, but in his own self-image as a "good" person. When reality crashes against this fantasy, the result is not moral triumph but farce. And yet, even in failure, Pralinsky is more human than villain—reminding us that the most dangerous illusions are often the ones we have about ourselves.

The Context of Russian Bureaucracy and Dostoevsky's Satirical Eye

To fully appreciate the significance of An Unpleasant Predicament, it helps to understand the social and political climate of Russia in the 1860s. The country was undergoing a period of profound transformation. The emancipation of the serfs in 1861 had radically altered the social hierarchy, while liberal reforms attempted to modernize the judiciary, education system, and local governance. At the same time, a bloated and inefficient bureaucracy continued to dominate civic life, producing legions of functionaries who were often more concerned with protocol than purpose.

Pralinsky is a creature of this world. He is steeped in the values of bureaucracy—hierarchy, decorum, procedure—but aspires to the values of a liberal idealist. Dostoevsky, ever suspicious of shallow liberalism and Western rationalism, uses this character to satirize the Russian intelligentsia's fascination with abstract moral systems and their detachment from the actual suffering and dignity of ordinary people.

Dostoevsky himself had complex views on reform and progress. While critical of the Tsarist state and its repressions, he was equally wary of utopian socialists and Westernizers who he believed ignored the spiritual and emotional needs of the Russian soul. In An Unpleasant Predicament, he exposes the contradiction between high-minded ideals and the messy, awkward realities of human life. Pralinsky's theory of equality fails not because it is wrong in principle, but because he is incapable of enacting it with humility and respect.

The setting of the wedding—a cramped, lower-middle-class apartment—serves as a stage for this social critique. Here, Dostoevsky offers a detailed and vivid portrayal of the discomfort, anxiety, and claustrophobia experienced by those on the margins of respectability. The groom's mother, the resentful guests, the trembling bride—all are sketched with empathy, revealing the strain that Pralinsky's intrusion places on their delicate social world. What he sees as a gesture of unity, they experience as a violation. This disconnect is the heart of the story's tragicomedy.

From a literary perspective, An Unpleasant Predicament aligns with a tradition of Russian satirical storytelling dating back to Gogol, whose influence is palpable in the grotesque comedy and exaggerated bureaucracy depicted here. Yet Dostoevsky brings a deeper psychological and moral dimension to the satire. Where Gogol revels in absurdity, Dostoevsky is more interested in the ethical confusion that lies beneath it.

In this way, the story functions as a kind of microcosm for Dostoevsky's larger project: to explore the conflict between ideology and experience, between appearance and reality, and between the desire to do good and the inability to escape self-delusion. It may be comedic, but it is comedy with teeth—and it leaves the reader with a sense of unease, even after the laughter fades.

The Lasting Power of Dostoevsky's Social Satire

Though it is rarely discussed alongside Dostoevsky's great novels, An Unpleasant Predicament is a quintessential example of his skill as a satirist and psychologist. It shows that even outside the epic sweep of his major works, Dostoevsky could deliver precise, scathing, and emotionally resonant critiques of human behavior.

The story is especially relevant in today's world, where questions of social status, performative virtue, and inequality continue to dominate public discourse. Pralinsky is a timeless figure—the well-meaning but tone-deaf official, the self-righteous do-gooder who confuses moral gestures with moral substance. His failure is not merely personal, but emblematic of a wider social blindness: the inability of those in power to see those beneath them as real, complex human beings.

What gives the story its lasting power is not just its humor, but its moral complexity. Dostoevsky refuses to offer simple answers. Pralinsky is neither villain nor hero. He is, rather, a man trying to be good in a way that flatters his own vanity. His failure is not due to malice but to a lack of self-awareness, a flaw that many readers will recognize in themselves. In this, Dostoevsky issues both a warning and an invitation: to examine our motivations more closely, to confront the uncomfortable truths beneath our most generous impulses, and to recognize that genuine human connection requires not just good intentions, but humility, empathy, and the courage to relinquish control.

This modern translation seeks to preserve the story's sharp wit and psychological insight while making Dostoevsky's prose more fluid and accessible to contemporary readers. The goal is not to simplify the story, but to allow its humor and depth to shine through without the linguistic barriers of 19th-century Russian formalism. In doing so, this version aims to reintroduce An Unpleasant Predicament as one of Dostoevsky's most engaging and instructive short works.

In conclusion, An Unpleasant Predicament is far more than an amusing anecdote—it is a sophisticated social satire that cuts to the heart of human folly. Through the tragicomic journey of one man's misguided attempt at moral heroism, Dostoevsky reveals the fragile ego beneath our most noble ideals and the chaos that can erupt when theory meets reality. It is a story that asks us to laugh not just at others, but at ourselves—and in doing so, to grow a little wiser.

An Unpleasant Predicament

This rather unpleasant and peculiar incident unfolded during a period when the regeneration of our cherished fatherland was taking its first vigorous strides, and the fervent ambitions of her valiant sons were propelling them toward new hopes and grand destinies. The era was marked by a blend of uncontainable enthusiasm and an almost childlike, endearing impulsiveness. It was on one winter evening of that transformative epoch, between the hours of eleven and midnight, that three highly respectable gentlemen found themselves in the elegant drawing room of a handsome, two-storey residence on the Petersburg Side. The setting was one of refinement, with furnishings exuding luxury and taste. These gentlemen, each of whom held the rank of general, were seated comfortably in plush, inviting armchairs around a small table. Their conversation, conducted in low, measured tones, revolved around a most edifying and engaging topic.

As they spoke, they sipped champagne from crystal glasses, the bottle resting nearby in a silver stand encased in ice. The host of the evening, Stepan Nikiforovitch Nikiforov, was a privy councillor and a man of precise habits. He was an old bachelor, sixty-five years of age, who had chosen this occasion to celebrate two milestones: his recent acquisition of a fine house and, somewhat unexpectedly, his birthday—an event he had rarely acknowledged in previous years. The celebration, however, was intentionally modest. Only two guests graced his evening, both of whom were former colleagues and subordinates: Semyon Ivanovitch Shipulenko, an actual civil councillor, and another of the same rank, Ivan Ilyitch Pralinsky.

The evening had commenced with tea at nine, transitioning soon after to wine. The guests, well aware of Stepan Nikiforovitch's preference for punctuality, knew they would be departing precisely at half-past eleven. It was in keeping with the host's lifelong devotion to routine. But before delving into the nuances of the evening, a few words about the host are in order.

Stepan Nikiforovitch's career had begun humbly, as a petty clerk, devoid of connections or privilege. Over forty-five years, he had quietly but determinedly climbed the ranks, always mindful of his limitations and never allowing ambition to blind him to his capacities. His aspirations were measured; he desired neither glory nor monumental achievement, contenting himself instead with a modest accumulation of respect and stability.

In character, he was a man of quiet intellect who shunned displays of wit or brilliance. Honesty was his guiding principle, though it must be said that he had never faced a situation that truly tested his moral fibre. He remained a bachelor, not for lack of opportunity, but because his nature was fundamentally self-contained. Averse to sloppiness of any kind, be it in appearance, habits, or emotion, he had come to regard enthusiasm itself as a form of untidiness. Over the years, this disposition had deepened, leading him to embrace a life of indulgent solitude, punctuated only by the ticking of his dining-room clock—a sound he found both soothing and companionable.

Physically, he was well-preserved, younger in appearance than his age might suggest, and scrupulously proper in his demeanor. His position, though not particularly demanding, allowed him to preside over proceedings and sign important documents, tasks he performed with an air of calm authority. His reputation as a "first-rate man" was unchallenged, and his only indulgence—his one great desire—had been to own a home befitting his station. That dream had recently been realized when he purchased a house on the Petersburg Side, a property complete with a garden and an air of genteel elegance. The distance from the city center suited him; it reduced the likelihood of uninvited guests. For transportation, he relied on his handsome chocolate-colored carriage, driven by Mihey, a coachman of impeccable reliability, and drawn by a pair of sturdy, well-kept horses. All this had been acquired through decades of careful saving, and his heart swelled with pride at the accomplishment.

This sense of contentment inspired him to extend an invitation to his two guests, a rare gesture. Stepan Nikiforovitch had even entertained a practical motive for one of his visitors. The lower floor of his newly purchased home, identical in layout to his own, was unoccupied, and he hoped to persuade Semyon Ivanovitch Shipulenko to rent it. Twice during the evening, he had broached the subject, but Semyon Ivanovitch had remained noncommittal, responding with nothing more than polite indifference.

Semyon Ivanovitch himself was a man of steady temperament and meticulous habits. A long career had honed his skills in navigating bureaucratic complexities. His austere demeanor, complemented by his dark hair and slightly jaundiced complexion, gave him an air of severity. Married and firmly rooted in his domestic life, he ruled his household with an iron hand and approached his professional duties with a similar resolve. Though not particularly moved by the wave of reforms sweeping through the country, he maintained a skeptical detachment, regarding them as distractions to his well-established routines.

The third gentleman, Ivan Ilyitch Pralinsky, was of a different breed altogether. A relatively young general at forty-three, he carried himself with the confidence of a man accustomed to admiration. Tall, impeccably dressed, and bearing a distinguished order on his chest, he exuded charm and vitality. Yet, beneath this polished exterior lay a man of contradictions. Born into privilege and accustomed to luxury, Ivan Ilyitch had navigated his career with a blend of ambition and self-assurance. He dreamed of greatness, of carving out a legacy that would endure, and while he occasionally questioned his own capabilities, he quickly dismissed such doubts, buoyed by an unwavering belief in his potential.

As the evening progressed, Ivan Ilyitch grew increasingly animated. Fuelled by champagne, he launched into a spirited critique of the reforms, directing much of his fervor at Stepan Nikiforovitch, whom he perceived as a symbol of outdated conservatism. The older man listened with a sly smile, allowing Ivan Ilyitch to exhaust himself in rhetoric. Meanwhile, Semyon Ivanovitch observed the exchange with a hint of amusement, his silence a subtle rebuke to Ivan Ilyitch's impassioned outbursts.

By the end of the evening, Ivan Ilyitch felt both exhilarated and unsettled. The sense of being subtly mocked by his companions gnawed at him, fuelling his determination to assert himself further. Yet, as the clock struck eleven-thirty and the guests prepared to leave, a sense of unease lingered, hinting that the evening's dynamics had unsettled more than just the champagne glasses.

"No, it was time, high time," Ivan Ilyitch continued passionately, his voice tinged with righteous conviction. "We have delayed this far too long, and, in my opinion, humanity must be our first priority—humanity toward those beneath us in rank, acknowledging that they, too, are human. It is humanity that will save us, guide us, and draw out the best in everyone."

From the corner of the room came a low, derisive chuckle—"He-he-he-he!"—courtesy of Semyon Ivanovitch.

"But why all this fervent lecturing?" Stepan Nikiforovitch interjected, his tone genial yet slightly bemused. A faint smile played on his lips as he added, "Forgive me, Ivan Ilyitch, but I still fail to grasp the crux of your argument. You are advocating humanity—by which, I take it, you mean love for one's fellow man?"

"Precisely, if you must summarize it that way," Ivan Ilyitch affirmed, though there was a hint of impatience in his voice. "I…"

"One moment!" Stepan Nikiforovitch raised a hand to interrupt him. "Surely, love for one's fellow man has always been a commendable sentiment. But if I understand correctly, what you are proposing goes beyond that. Love alone does not encapsulate the scope of the reform movement. We are confronting a deluge of issues: the peasantry, judicial reform, economic policies, government contracts, morality—the list is endless. These questions have the potential to provoke significant upheavals, so to speak. That, my dear friend, is where our concern lies—not simply with humanity alone."

"Indeed, it's a great deal more complex than that," Semyon Ivanovitch added, with a tone that bordered on condescension.

"I fully comprehend the complexity," Ivan Ilyitch retorted, his sarcasm cutting as he addressed Semyon Ivanovitch directly. "And I assure you, sir, I take great exception to the implication that my understanding of these matters is somehow less profound than yours. Allow me to clarify, Stepan Nikiforovitch, that you, too, have misunderstood me."

"That may very well be," Stepan Nikiforovitch replied mildly, arching his eyebrows in feigned confusion. "Do enlighten us, then."

"I assert, and will continue to assert," Ivan Ilyitch declared, his tone brimming with fiery conviction, "that humanity—extending down the hierarchical ladder, from high-ranking officials to the humblest peasants—

should serve as the cornerstone of all forthcoming reforms. It is humanity, in all its forms, that will underpin the transformation of society at large. Allow me to explain: If I, as a human being, treat another with respect and kindness, that generates trust. Trust fosters understanding. Understanding breeds unity, and unity—"

"Breeds love," Semyon Ivanovitch interrupted, his sardonic grin widening. "Or perhaps yet another syllogism?"

Ivan Ilyitch shot him a withering glare. "I fail to see what you find so amusing," he snapped. "What I am advocating is both logical and necessary. If we can build trust among all levels of society, we lay the foundation for progress. But that requires vision and courage—qualities I would not expect everyone to possess."

Stepan Nikiforovitch, who had been silently observing the exchange, finally spoke, his tone deliberately neutral. "I fear we would collapse under the weight of such aspirations," he remarked, almost to himself.

"What precisely do you mean by that?" Ivan Ilyitch asked, his irritation giving way to curiosity.

"I mean," Stepan Nikiforovitch replied slowly, "that the strain might prove too much for the system. It may simply be unsustainable."

"Ah, I see!" Ivan Ilyitch exclaimed, his voice tinged with irony. "You're suggesting, then, that we are like old wineskins trying to contain new wine? Well, I cannot speak for others, but I am confident that I, at least, am up to the challenge."

At that precise moment, the clock chimed half-past eleven. The sound seemed to break the tension in the room, prompting Semyon Ivanovitch to rise from his chair.

"One sits and sits," he remarked dryly, "but at some point, one must leave."

Before he could finish, however, Ivan Ilyitch had already stood, reaching for his elegant sable cap resting on the mantel. There was an air of affront about him, as though he had been slighted.

"And what of the flat, Semyon Ivanovitch?" Stepan Nikiforovitch inquired as he escorted his guests to the door. "Will you give it some thought?"

"I'll think it over," Semyon Ivanovitch replied curtly, adjusting his shabby raccoon coat. "I'll let you know soon."

Meanwhile, Ivan Ilyitch lingered by the doorway, clearly feeling overlooked. "Still discussing business, I see," he remarked in a tone that was meant to sound affable but carried an edge of reproach.

Stepan Nikiforovitch raised his eyebrows again but said nothing, leaving Ivan Ilyitch to interpret the silence as dismissal. They parted with a polite but cool exchange of handshakes.

Once outside, the two men descended the steps in silence. The disparity between Ivan Ilyitch's luxurious fur coat and Semyon Ivanovitch's threadbare attire was glaring, though neither man commented on it. When they reached the street, they discovered that Ivan Ilyitch's carriage was nowhere to be found.

"What is this nonsense?" Ivan Ilyitch exclaimed angrily. "Where is my carriage? What has Trifon done with it?"

The coachman for Semyon Ivanovitch's modest sledge shrugged indifferently. "He said something about attending a wedding nearby, sir," he offered. "But he promised to return quickly."

"That scoundrel!" Ivan Ilyitch fumed. "I'll make him pay for this! What nerve—leaving me stranded on a night like this."

"Would you care for a ride?" Semyon Ivanovitch offered with a smirk, though his tone was anything but sincere.

"Thank you, but no," Ivan Ilyitch replied icily. "Enjoy your journey."

As Semyon Ivanovitch drove off, Ivan Ilyitch set off on foot, his irritation mounting with every step. Yet as he walked, the biting cold and the serene beauty of the moonlit night began to temper his anger. The frost sparkled on the wooden pavement, and the stars seemed to twinkle just for him.

"Perhaps this is for the best," he mused. "A brisk walk will do me good. It serves as a lesson to Trifon, and it's not unpleasant to walk on such a night. How quaint these little houses are—clerks and tradesmen, no doubt, making their humble lives here."

Despite himself, Ivan Ilyitch felt his mood lift. The crisp air seemed to sharpen his thoughts, and he began to reflect again on his earlier argument. "Humanity," he thought. "The key to everything is humanity. Restore a man's dignity, give him a sense of worth, and he will thrive. It's such a simple, clear truth. Why couldn't they see it? Especially that smug Semyon Ivanovitch with his condescending smile."

As he continued down the street, Ivan Ilyitch found himself speaking aloud, weaving grand theories and elaborate arguments to an invisible audience. The night, so silent and vast, seemed to embrace his words, magnifying his conviction and lending a kind of poetic rhythm to his thoughts. By the time he reached the Great Prospect, his earlier frustrations had melted away, leaving only the comforting certainty of his own brilliance.

"'Flog him in the police station,' he said that deliberately, just to provoke me," Ivan Ilyitch muttered to himself, his stride quickening as if to outpace his own irritation. "What utter nonsense! Flogging? No, that's not my way. You can beat a man, but words—words can strike deeper, cut sharper, and linger longer. I'll punish Trifon with words, with reproaches he won't forget. Yes, that's the civilized approach. Flogging, after all, is an archaic method, h'm... though the debate over its morality is ongoing, h'm..."

His thoughts trailed off, distracted by the uneven pavement. "Damn this accursed city!" he exclaimed aloud as he stumbled slightly. "And this is supposed to be the capital? Enlightenment, progress—bah! A man could break his leg here!" He paused, rubbing his shin before continuing. "And as for Semyon Ivanovitch, what a smug, despicable face he has. Laughing at me earlier, mocking me when I said people would embrace one another in a moral sense. Well, why shouldn't they? They will embrace, and what's it to him? I wouldn't embrace him, though—I'd much rather embrace a peasant, someone simple, uncorrupted by pretension."

He stopped briefly to adjust his coat, then resumed his walk. "If I meet a peasant tonight, I shall talk to him," he resolved. "Perhaps I was unclear earlier. Maybe the wine muddled my words, as it often does. Yes, I must stop drinking. In the evening, you babble away, and by morning, you regret every word. Yet here I am, walking steadily enough. No, I'm not drunk; it's just that they're all scoundrels, every last one of them!"

Ivan Ilyitch's thoughts ebbed and flowed in fragments, the cool night air invigorating his mind. Soon, the rhythmic tapping of his boots on the wooden pavement began to calm him. His agitation softened into a reflective haze. Five minutes more, and he might have been entirely at peace—might even have felt drowsy—but then, faint strains of music reached his ears. He stopped abruptly, the lively melody pulling him from his reverie.

Across the street, in a dilapidated one-story wooden house, a celebration was in full swing. Violins scratched out a lively tune, a double bass rumbled steadily, and a flute shrieked its high-pitched contribution to what sounded like a quadrille. From within came the thud of feet on wooden floors, unmistakable evidence of energetic dancing. Outside, a small crowd had gathered—mostly women bundled in wadded pelisses and kerchiefs, craning their necks to peer through a crack in the shutters. The air was alive with the unmistakable hum of festivity.

Curious, Ivan Ilyitch crossed the street, his expensive fur coat catching the moonlight as he approached a policeman stationed nearby. "Whose house is this, brother?" he asked, his tone carrying the authority of his rank. As he spoke, he casually flung open his coat just enough to reveal the glinting decoration pinned to his chest.

The policeman immediately straightened, recognizing the insignia. "This house, your Honour? It belongs to the registration clerk, Pseldonimov."

"Pseldonimov?" Ivan Ilyitch repeated, the name vaguely familiar. "And what's the occasion? A wedding?"

"Yes, your Honour," the policeman confirmed. "He's marrying the daughter of a titular councillor, Mlekopitaev. The house comes with the bride."

"So, it's Pseldonimov's house now, not Mlekopitaev's?"

"Exactly, sir. It was Mlekopitaev's, but now it's Pseldonimov's."

"H'm, interesting." Ivan Ilyitch nodded thoughtfully. "I ask because Pseldonimov is one of my subordinates. I'm a general in his department."

"Indeed, your Excellency," the policeman replied, drawing himself up even straighter, clearly eager to impress.

Ivan Ilyitch stood still, his thoughts swirling. Pseldonimov… yes, the name rang a bell. He pictured a young man—thin, awkward, with tufts of flaxen hair and a nose too large for his face. His uniform had been threadbare, and his trousers so ill-fitting as to verge on indecency. Ivan Ilyitch recalled briefly considering a Christmas bonus for the poor fellow—ten roubles, perhaps, to improve his wardrobe—but something in Pseldonimov's austere, almost repellant demeanor had made him reconsider. Yet here he was now, hosting a wedding in a house of his own, with a dowry of four hundred roubles and property attached. The juxtaposition of the surnames Pseldonimov and Mlekopitaev had even elicited a wry comment from Ivan Ilyitch when he approved the marriage request weeks ago.

Lost in thought, Ivan Ilyitch felt a surge of conflicting emotions. "So here I stand," he mused, "outside the home of my subordinate on the happiest day of his life. And what if I were to go in? What would Pseldonimov think? He'd be terrified at first, of course—frozen with embarrassment. But why should he be? I am no ordinary general. If I entered, it would not be to scold or to intimidate, but to inspire, to demonstrate the principles of humanity I've so fervently advocated."

He began pacing, his thoughts racing. "Yes, humanity! That's the cornerstone of everything. Stepan Nikiforovitch scoffed at me earlier, but here's a chance to prove my point. A gesture like this—stepping into the home of a clerk earning ten roubles a month—would be revolutionary, a true act of moral courage. It would unsettle conventions, challenge the old ways, and yet… it would be beautiful, patriarchal, even sublime. Others might see it as folly, but I would transform it into a noble act, a symbol of progress and unity."

The music swelled again, and Ivan Ilyitch stopped in his tracks. "Shall I go in?" he asked himself. "Shall I show them all what it means to lead by example? Yes, I shall!" His resolve hardened, and with a determined stride, he moved toward the brightly lit house, his mind already composing the magnanimous speech he would deliver to the astonished guests.

"Here I am, standing outside this house, and what if I were to step inside?" Ivan Ilyitch mused, his mind racing ahead of him, building the scenario brick by brick. "Of course, the moment I walk in, they would stop everything. The dancing would halt, the music would falter, and everyone would stare at me in disbelief. It would be like a scene out of a play—the grand general descending into the modest home of his subordinate. Their jaws would drop, their eyes would go wide, and for a moment, they'd all be frozen, unsure whether to bow, to run, or simply faint from shock."

He allowed himself a wry smile at the imagined scene. "But then I'd take charge, wouldn't I? I'd go straight up to Pseldonimov, who'd likely be shaking in his boots, and I'd flash him the warmest, most affable smile. In the simplest, most casual tone, I'd say, 'Well, my dear fellow, I've just come from his Excellency Stepan Nikiforovitch's. You know, just around the corner.' Then, lightly, with a touch of humor, I'd recount my little adventure with Trifon. That would break the ice. From Trifon, I'd segue seamlessly into how I decided to walk here on foot—'And then I heard music,' I'd say. 'So I asked a policeman what the commotion was and learned it was your wedding! Well, how could I not stop by? I thought to myself, let me see how my clerks celebrate such a joyous occasion.'"

He chuckled at his own cleverness, imagining Pseldonimov's reaction. "Would he dare to turn me out? Impossible! The very thought! No, he'd be half out of his mind with joy and terror. He'd rush to find me the best chair in the room, his hands trembling as he struggled to decide whether to bow or salute. Delight would overwhelm him, and for a moment, he'd be completely beside himself.

"And what could be simpler, more elegant than such an action on my part? Why did I go in? Ah, now that's the deeper question. That's the moral crux of the matter, isn't it? The essence of the act."

Ivan Ilyitch paused in his mental rehearsal, savoring the imagined triumph. "Let's see, what would happen next? They'd sit me with their most important guest— a titular councillor, perhaps, or some retired captain with a ruddy nose. I'd make polite conversation, of course. Compliment the bride, encourage the guests to continue enjoying themselves, urge them not to let my presence disrupt the festivities. I'd crack a few jokes, laugh heartily, and be utterly charming. I'm always charming when I'm in the mood for it. Yes, I'd blend right in, not as a general, but as a gentleman. That's key."

He frowned for a moment, reconsidering. "But then again, I am not just any gentleman. Morally speaking, my presence there carries a different weight. It's symbolic. They'd sense that, of course. They'd understand that this is no ordinary visit. My actions would resonate, would awaken something noble in them. I'd stay, oh, half an hour, perhaps an hour at most. Certainly not long enough to disrupt their supper preparations. I'd have a single glass of wine, toast to their happiness, and politely decline any further hospitality. 'Business,' I'd say. Just that one word. And with it, they'd all straighten their backs, their faces suddenly solemn with respect. They'd be reminded of the vast gulf between us—earth and sky, as it were."

He nodded to himself, satisfied. "Of course, I'd soften it immediately, smiling and joking once more, restoring the easy atmosphere. I might even tease the bride, hinting that in nine months' time I'd be back to stand as godfather to their first child. That would bring a roar of laughter from the guests. The bride would blush, I'd kiss her forehead with a fatherly air, and then, with a final blessing, I'd take my leave."

He pictured the aftermath with growing satisfaction. "The next day, the whole office would be buzzing. They'd whisper about how the general himself attended Pseldonimov's wedding. By then, I'd be my usual stern, exacting self, but they'd see me differently. They'd know my heart, my true nature. 'He's strict, but he's an angel of a man,' they'd say. I'd have won them over, body and soul, with one simple act that none of those old fogies like Stepan Nikiforovitch would ever dream of attempting."

His imagination ran further. "And Pseldonimov! He'd tell the story to his children, who'd tell it to their children. For generations, they'd pass down the tale of how the great general graced their humble wedding with his presence. It would become a family legend, a sacred story. By elevating him in this way, I'd be restoring his dignity, giving him something to hold onto. A man who earns ten roubles a month! To him, this act would be transformative."

He strode forward, his resolve hardening. "If I do this five, ten times—who knows?—my name will be imprinted on their hearts. They'll remember me as a true leader, a man of the people. Popularity like that— why, it could change everything. Who knows where it might lead?" His heart swelled with the possibilities as he approached the house, ready to transform his vision into reality.

The thoughts that had surged through Ivan Ilyitch's mind in mere moments might have remained as harmless musings, and he could have walked home quietly, putting Stepan Nikiforovitch to shame in his imagination alone. Such a course of action would have been prudent, even wise. But unfortunately, fate had conspired against him in this eccentric moment.

As he stood there, the smug, disdainful expressions of Stepan Nikiforovitch and Semyon Ivanovitch seemed to materialize before him, vivid and mocking.

"We shall break down!" Stepan Nikiforovitch had sneered, his voice dripping with condescension.

"He-he-he!" Semyon Ivanovitch had added with his signature sardonic chuckle, the one that grated on Ivan Ilyitch like nails on glass.

"We'll see who breaks down!" Ivan Ilyitch muttered aloud, his face flushing hot with defiance and a sudden surge of adrenaline. Without hesitation, he stepped off the pavement, crossed the street, and made his way toward the house where Pseldonimov's wedding celebration was in full swing.

His decision felt monumental, almost preordained. The stars seemed to carry him forward as he strode through the open gate with resolute purpose. A shaggy little sheepdog barked hoarsely at his legs, more out of duty than conviction, but Ivan Ilyitch dismissed it with an almost contemptuous nudge of his foot. The dog retreated, and he pressed onward, following a wooden plank path to the covered porch. Three creaky wooden steps led him to a narrow entryway, dimly lit by a feeble tallow candle.

The moment he stepped inside, misfortune struck. His left foot, still clad in its galosh, sank into something cold and gelatinous. Glancing down, he realized with horror that he had trampled a beautifully prepared galantine. Around it were other dishes: more jelly, and what appeared to be blancmange, all carefully placed to cool. Ivan Ilyitch froze. For a fleeting moment, he considered retreating, slinking away before anyone noticed. But pride intervened. No, he couldn't stoop to that. Instead, he wiped his galosh on the wooden floorboards, attempting to erase the evidence of his clumsiness.

He fumbled for the felt-covered door and, upon finding it, entered the house. The small anteroom he stepped into was crowded with coats, scarves, and galoshes. On the other side of the room, a makeshift band of street musicians—a quartet consisting of two violins, a flute, and a double bass—were energetically sawing out the final figure of a quadrille. Their unpolished music spilled through an open door into a smoke-filled drawing room, where laughter, shouting, and the rhythmic thud of dancing feet created a cacophony of joyous chaos.

Ivan Ilyitch stood for a moment, taking in the scene. The room, though small and crowded with about thirty guests, pulsed with an exuberant energy. The air was thick with tobacco smoke and the faint odor of wax. Amid the swirling dresses and animated faces, a blue scarf brushed against his nose as a medical student, wild-haired and red-faced with excitement, barreled past, nearly knocking into him. The atmosphere was one of unrestrained revelry, but it felt utterly alien to Ivan Ilyitch, who remained rooted near the door, his cap in hand.

For a few seconds, no one noticed him. Then, as the quadrille ended, the very reaction Ivan Ilyitch had envisioned earlier on the pavement unfolded with uncanny accuracy. A ripple of murmurs spread through the crowd. Faces turned toward him, one by one, eyes wide with surprise. The music stopped; the laughter faded. Gradually, an awkward silence settled over the room as an invisible line seemed to form between the general and the guests. They edged back slightly, creating a widening gap on the floor littered with sweet wrappers and cigarette butts.

From the midst of the gathering, a figure hesitantly emerged—a young man in uniform with a hooked nose and a mop of flaxen hair. It was Pseldonimov, his expression one of pure terror. He shuffled forward with a hunched posture, his every movement radiating uncertainty. His face bore the same look of timid dread one might see on a dog summoned by its master for punishment.

"Good evening, Pseldonimov. Do you know me?" Ivan Ilyitch asked, his voice faltering slightly as he realized how awkward the situation had become. The moment the words left his mouth, he regretted them. The question sounded both unnecessary and clumsy.

"Y-your Excellency!" Pseldonimov stammered, his voice barely audible.

"Indeed. I happened to be in the neighborhood," Ivan Ilyitch began, trying to sound casual. "I thought

I'd drop in and congratulate you. I heard the music and realized it must be your wedding. Naturally, I couldn't resist paying my respects."

But Pseldonimov stood frozen, his wide-eyed confusion bordering on panic. His mind seemed incapable of processing what was happening. The sight of his superior at his modest wedding was so incongruous that he appeared to suspect a cruel joke.

"You won't turn me out, I suppose?" Ivan Ilyitch added with a forced laugh, trying to lighten the mood. "Surely, you'd welcome a visitor—even an uninvited one."

Pseldonimov opened his mouth but said nothing, his face a mask of bewilderment. Ivan Ilyitch's discomfort deepened. He could feel the weight of every pair of eyes in the room fixed upon him, scrutinizing his every gesture.

"I'm not in the way, am I?" he ventured, his voice barely above a whisper now. "If so, I can leave...."

A faint tremor appeared at the corner of his mouth, betraying his growing unease. He stood there, a towering figure of authority, reduced to a state of near humiliation by the very people he had intended to inspire.

Pseldonimov, though visibly flustered, began to recover himself. His expression shifted from frozen panic to hurried deference, though his movements were still awkward and jerky.

"Good heavens, your Excellency ... such an honor!" he stammered, bowing repeatedly. "Please, graciously sit down, your Excellency!" He gestured with both hands toward a sofa, hastily shifting a small table away from its front to make room, evidently trying to create an inviting space.

Ivan Ilyitch, inwardly relieved by the semblance of normalcy returning, sank into the sofa. Almost immediately, someone darted forward to push the table back into position before him. As he settled, he became acutely aware of the peculiar dynamic in the room. He was the only one seated; everyone else—guests, musicians, even the servants peering in from the hallway—stood watching him. This silent attention felt suffocating, as though he were on display. The stiffness of the gathering confirmed that his unanticipated arrival had unsettled everyone.

Yet it was not the moment to begin making lighthearted conversation. He could sense the crowd needed reassurance, and he himself was grappling with a growing awkwardness. Pseldonimov stood just a few feet away, still bent at an angle as though perpetually mid-bow, his nervousness rendering him incapable of any expression beyond pure reverence.

Then, suddenly, a small figure emerged from the corner of the room. A wave of relief swept over Ivan Ilyitch as he recognized the individual: Akim Petrovitch Zubikov, the head clerk from his office. Though their relationship had never gone beyond the formalities of a superior and subordinate, Ivan Ilyitch had always considered Zubikov dependable and businesslike. At this moment, Zubikov's presence felt like a godsend—a familiar and steady face in a sea of confusion.

With newfound enthusiasm, Ivan Ilyitch rose from the sofa and extended his hand—not just two fingers, but his entire hand—in a gesture of respect and cordiality. Akim Petrovitch, visibly taken aback but deeply flattered, took his superior's hand in both of his own with almost comical reverence. This small but deliberate act transformed the atmosphere. The tension in the room lessened, and Ivan Ilyitch sensed that he had regained a measure of control over the situation.

"Ah, Akim Petrovitch!" Ivan Ilyitch exclaimed warmly, his voice steadier now. "It is good to see you here."

With Zubikov's presence serving as a stabilizing force, Ivan Ilyitch shifted his focus. Pseldonimov, though still hovering nearby, was effectively sidelined.

This allowed the general to direct his remarks primarily toward the head clerk, using him as a bridge to communicate with the room. Pseldonimov, now relegated to the role of an onlooker, continued to stand rigidly, his hands nervously fidgeting with the cuffs of his ill-fitting jacket.

"Imagine my surprise," Ivan Ilyitch began, his tone taking on an almost theatrical quality, "to find myself here tonight. A curious chain of events brought me to your wedding, Pseldonimov. Truly, it seems fate itself intended me to join in your celebration!"

Pseldonimov's mouth opened slightly as though to respond, but no words came out. Ivan Ilyitch pressed on, now addressing Zubikov directly, as if to draw focus away from the groom's evident discomfort.

"I was just at the home of Stepan Nikiforovitch Nikiforov," he explained, leaning back slightly to adopt a more conversational tone. "You know of him, of course—the esteemed privy councillor and a man of no small reputation. Today was both his birthday and a housewarming for his new residence—a splendid property, I must say."

Zubikov nodded vigorously, his entire demeanor one of deferential agreement. The crowd, meanwhile, listened with a mixture of awe and curiosity. Ivan Ilyitch could feel their attention turning toward him, their initial shock gradually morphing into interest.

"I must say, the evening was delightful," he continued, allowing a faint smile to play across his lips. "We had champagne, excellent conversation, and even a bit of friendly debate. But then—" He paused for effect, glancing around the room as though letting the suspense build. "Then, just as I was leaving, I discovered that my coachman, Trifon, had gone missing—along with my carriage!"

A collective gasp rippled through the audience. Even Pseldonimov, despite his wooden demeanor, widened his eyes slightly in surprise.

"Yes, gone without a trace!" Ivan Ilyitch exclaimed, leaning forward slightly to emphasize his words. "And do you know why? The scoundrel had taken the carriage to attend a wedding—this very wedding, as it turns out!"

This revelation elicited murmurs and whispers from the assembled guests. Some exchanged glances, while others looked toward Pseldonimov as though expecting him to offer an explanation. Zubikov chuckled politely, clearly eager to match the general's tone.

"But no matter," Ivan Ilyitch said, waving his hand dismissively. "What better reason could there be for such a breach of duty than to celebrate the union of two fine individuals?" He gestured vaguely toward Pseldonimov, whose face reddened under the scrutiny.

Encouraged by the faint ripple of laughter from the crowd, Ivan Ilyitch pressed forward. "And so, with no carriage to be found, I decided to walk. The night was beautiful, after all—clear skies, crisp air, and the faint sound of music guiding me here. And now that I am here, I must say, the atmosphere is delightful. You've gathered quite the lively company, Pseldonimov!"

"He-he-he! To be sure!" Zubikov chimed in obligingly, his laughter more enthusiastic than the situation warranted.

Ivan Ilyitch smiled, but his eyes flicked briefly to Pseldonimov, who still had not managed even a faint grin. The groom's stony expression grated on his nerves, but he pressed on, determined not to let the moment slip from his control.

"If I may say so," Ivan Ilyitch added, his tone becoming almost paternal, "this is a night to remember, a true testament to joy and the bonds that unite us. Let us raise our spirits and celebrate with the warmth and camaraderie befitting such a momentous occasion."

As he concluded, a faint cheer rose from the crowd. The ice had begun to thaw, though Pseldonimov's rigid posture remained a frustrating reminder of the challenges Ivan Ilyitch faced in fully winning over the room. Still, he felt a growing confidence that his impromptu visit would, in the end, be seen as a gesture of goodwill and magnanimity.

"I thought it would be a pleasant surprise to drop in and see my clerk on this momentous occasion. After all, I'm not one to intrude where I'm not wanted," Ivan Ilyitch began, his tone light but tinged with unease. "If my presence is a disruption, just say the word, and I'll leave. I assure you, I came only to offer my congratulations and see how the celebration was going."

His words seemed to send a ripple through the room. Akim Petrovitch, standing awkwardly nearby, cast him a mawkishly sweet look, as if silently reassuring him, "How could your Excellency ever be in the way?" Around the room, the other guests began to stir, their stiff postures loosening slightly. Almost imperceptibly, the atmosphere shifted. Several women ventured to take their seats, a promising signal of the tension easing. The bolder ones fanned themselves with their handkerchiefs, and one particularly daring woman, clad in a worn velvet dress, made a loud comment, seemingly to assert her ease in the general's presence. Her companion, an officer, attempted to respond in kind but quickly retreated into silence upon realizing their voices were the only ones breaking the quiet.

The men—government clerks and a smattering of students—exchanged glances, as if daring each other to relax. A few cleared their throats, shuffled their feet, and moved hesitantly about the room. Yet, despite the faint thaw, there was a palpable undercurrent of suspicion. The unwelcome guest had disrupted their merriment, and many regarded him with thinly veiled hostility. The officer, perhaps trying to save face, edged closer to the table, his expression a mixture of irritation and curiosity.

"But tell me, my friend," Ivan Ilyitch said, turning to Pseldonimov with what he hoped was an affable smile, "may I have the honor of knowing your full name?"

"Porfiry Petrovitch, your Excellency," Pseldonimov replied stiffly, his posture as straight as if he were standing at attention.

"Well, Porfiry Petrovitch," Ivan Ilyitch continued, his tone growing warmer, "introduce me to your bride, won't you? I'd like to meet the lady of the hour." He began to rise, but Pseldonimov, clearly flustered, darted toward the drawing room.

The bride, who had been standing near the door, quickly slipped out of sight as soon as she heard herself mentioned. Moments later, Pseldonimov reappeared, leading her by the hand. The guests parted like a wave to make room for them, their eyes riveted on the scene.

Ivan Ilyitch rose to his feet and greeted her with a polished, aristocratic half-bow, his most charming smile firmly in place.

"Delighted to make your acquaintance," he said, his voice smooth and affable. "And especially on such a joyful occasion as this."

His graciousness elicited a soft murmur from the crowd. A woman in the velvet dress leaned toward her neighbor and whispered audibly, "Charmé!" adding a touch of theatricality to her exclamation.

The bride was a petite, delicate young woman, likely no older than seventeen. Pale, with a sharp little nose and a small, pointed face, she possessed an understated prettiness that contrasted starkly with her thin, almost birdlike frame. Her quick, observant eyes betrayed no shyness; instead, they met Ivan Ilyitch's gaze with a steady, almost defiant stare. Her demeanor suggested that she was not easily overawed, even by the likes of a general.

"She is quite pretty," Ivan Ilyitch remarked in a lower tone, as though confiding to Pseldonimov but ensuring the bride could hear. He hoped the compliment would elicit a blush or a shy smile, but her expression remained impassive. Her only response was a perfunctory nod, and her silence created an awkward void.

"An interesting couple," Ivan Ilyitch thought, glancing from the bride to her groom. "But this silence—it's unbearable." He asked the bride a few polite questions, but her answers were monosyllabic at best. Her reticence, coupled with Pseldonimov's wooden demeanor, left him feeling increasingly out of place.

"My dear friends," he said at last, addressing the entire room in an effort to regain control of the situation, "surely I haven't disrupted your enjoyment? Do let me know if I've been an inconvenience."

Sweat was beginning to bead on his palms, a sensation he found deeply unsettling.

"No, no, your Excellency," the officer spoke up, his tone polite but tinged with defensiveness. "We were just cooling off for a moment. We'll be resuming shortly."

The bride turned toward the officer with evident approval. Ivan Ilyitch noted the exchange with growing irritation. Pseldonimov, meanwhile, stood motionless, his hooked nose and hunched posture giving him the air of a valet awaiting his master's next command. The comparison sprang unbidden to Ivan Ilyitch's mind, and he found it maddening. "Is he truly incapable of even the smallest gesture of warmth?" he thought.

Suddenly, the crowd shifted, and a new figure entered the room. She was a stout, middle-aged woman, plainly dressed in her Sunday best. A large shawl was wrapped snugly around her shoulders, and a slightly crooked cap adorned her head, suggesting she was unaccustomed to wearing such finery. In her hands, she carried a modest tray bearing a single bottle of champagne and two glasses.

"Your Excellency," she began, her voice warm and unpretentious, "we are humbled and honored by your presence at my son's wedding. Please, do us the kindness of toasting the young couple's health. It would mean so much to us."

Her rosy cheeks and kind, unassuming smile were a balm to Ivan Ilyitch's frazzled nerves. The sincerity of her gesture seemed to cut through the awkwardness that had been suffocating the room. He felt a surge of gratitude and relief as he accepted her offering.

"Madam," he said, rising to his feet, "it is I who am honored to share in this joyful occasion. Let us indeed drink to the happiness of this fine young couple."

The room began to stir again, and for the first time that evening, Ivan Ilyitch sensed that he might yet salvage the situation.

"So you are the mo-ther of your so-on?" Ivan Ilyitch inquired, rising from the sofa with exaggerated courtesy, his syllables drawn out in a tone of mock ceremony that barely masked his unease.

"Yes, indeed, your Excellency," Pseldonimov stammered, craning his neck and thrusting forward his long, thin nose in a gesture of eager compliance. His discomfort was palpable, but he tried to compensate with deference.

"Ah! Delighted—truly de-light-ed to make your acquaintance," Ivan Ilyitch replied, bowing slightly toward the woman.

"Please, your Excellency, do not refuse us this honor," the mother entreated, her voice warm and laden with earnest hospitality.

"With the greatest pleasure," Ivan Ilyitch responded, attempting to match her warmth. The tray she carried was carefully placed on the table, and Pseldonimov, in a sudden burst of activity, scrambled to pour the wine. Ivan Ilyitch remained standing as he accepted the glass, lifting it with a ceremonial flourish.

"I am particularly, particularly glad on this special occasion," he began, addressing the bride and groom with a labored air of geniality, "that I have the opportunity ... the privilege ... to testify before all of you my heartfelt wishes. As your chief, I must express my sincerest congratulations. Madam," he said, turning to the bride with a strained smile, "and you, Porfiry, my dear friend, I wish you endless happiness and the fullest blessings for many, many long years."

With an almost theatrical flourish, Ivan Ilyitch drained the glass, his seventh of the evening. The gesture, intended to convey warmth and ease, only underscored the growing tension in the room. Pseldonimov stood motionless, his expression as grave as ever, perhaps even edging toward a faint sullenness. The general felt a wave of irritation rising in him.

"And that officer," Ivan Ilyitch thought bitterly, casting a sideways glance at the man in uniform who stood rigid and silent in the corner, "couldn't even muster a simple 'hurrah!' It would have lightened the mood, it really would have."

At that moment, the old woman turned to Akim Petrovitch, the head clerk, her tone a mix of maternal pride and gentle pleading. "And you too, Akim Petrovitch, drink to their health. You are his superior, after all. He works under you. Look after my boy, I beg you, as a mother would. Please don't forget us in the future, our kind and good friend."

"How charmingly earnest these old Russian women are," Ivan Ilyitch mused, his irritation momentarily displaced by a genuine appreciation for her sincerity. "They have a way of warming the heart. Such a lively spirit she has! I've always admired the simplicity of the people."

At that moment, a second tray appeared, carried in by a young maid whose crisp cotton dress rustled audibly as she moved. She approached with visible effort, balancing an enormous tray laden with plates of apples, sugared sweets, meringues, walnuts, and other confections. Ivan Ilyitch immediately recognized the gesture: the tray, previously enjoyed by all the guests, had now been brought over as a special offering for him.

"Do not disdain our humble fare, your Excellency," the old woman said, bowing low once more. "What little we have, we are pleased to offer you."

"Delighted, truly delighted!" Ivan Ilyitch exclaimed, taking a walnut from the tray with evident pleasure. He cracked it expertly between his fingers, determined to appear approachable and at ease. Internally, he resolved to secure his popularity at all costs.

A sudden giggle interrupted his thoughts. It came from the bride. Ivan Ilyitch turned toward her, a hopeful smile spreading across his face.

"What is it?" he asked, encouraged by this unexpected sign of animation.

"It's Ivan Kostenkinitch," she answered, lowering her gaze with an embarrassed smile. "He's making me laugh."

Following her gaze, Ivan Ilyitch spotted a flaxen-haired young man seated awkwardly at the far end of the sofa, whispering something to the bride. The youth stood up abruptly, clearly flustered but attempting to compose himself.

"I was telling the lady about a 'dream book,' your Excellency," he mumbled, his voice tinged with nervousness, as though apologizing for his very existence.

"A dream book, you say?" Ivan Ilyitch inquired with polite condescension.

"Yes, your Excellency. It's a new literary one. I was explaining to the lady that dreaming of Mr. Panaev supposedly foretells spilling coffee on one's shirtfront."

"How innocent," Ivan Ilyitch thought, suppressing a sigh of annoyance. The young man, oblivious to the general's growing impatience, flushed a deep red, clearly delighted to have spoken.

Before Ivan Ilyitch could respond, another voice chimed in, its tone confident and assertive. "There's something far more amusing than that," said a young man in a white waistcoat, holding his hat with an air of studied nonchalance. "They say Mr. Kraevsky is writing articles for a new encyclopedia. Satirical ones, at that."

This newcomer, evidently a staff writer for the satirical journal The Firebrand, carried himself with an air of superiority that Ivan Ilyitch found particularly irksome. The general noted his casual demeanor and uninvited familiarity with growing disapproval.

The flaxen-haired youth, eager to reclaim attention, added hastily, "The joke is that Mr. Kraevsky supposedly thinks 'satirical' should be spelled with a 'y' instead of an 'i.' That's why it's funny, your Excellency."

But his attempt to amuse fell flat. Ivan Ilyitch's restrained reaction conveyed that he was unimpressed, and the young man, sensing his misstep, blushed furiously and sank into a morose silence for the rest of the evening.

The satirical writer, however, seemed intent on staying close to Ivan Ilyitch, positioning himself with an air of camaraderie that struck the general as unseemly.

Desperate to shift the conversation, Ivan Ilyitch turned to Pseldonimov with a question that had been nagging at him. "Porfiry, tell me—why are you called Pseldonimov instead of Pseudonimov? Surely your name ought to be the latter?"

Pseldonimov looked confused but answered dutifully, "I cannot say for certain, your Excellency."

"It must have been a clerical error," Akim Petrovitch interjected helpfully. "When his father joined the service, the name was likely written down incorrectly in the official documents, and it's remained Pseldonimov ever since."

"Ah, I see," Ivan Ilyitch said, though inwardly he felt more exasperated than ever. "How utterly trivial."

"Un-doubted-ly," Ivan Ilyitch said with deliberate emphasis, letting the word roll off his tongue with the warmth of one offering a sage observation, "un-doubted-ly. Consider, Pseldonimov comes directly from the literary word pseudonym, signifying something, while Pseldonimov—well, it amounts to nothing at all."

"That is due to foolishness," Akim Petrovitch interjected, as though providing a footnote to a lecture.

"What precisely do you mean by 'due to foolishness'?" Ivan Ilyitch asked, raising his eyebrows, though his tone remained indulgent.

"The Russian common folk," Akim Petrovitch elaborated, "often alter letters out of ignorance, and pronounce words in their own peculiar way. For instance, they say nevalid instead of invalid."

"Ah, yes, nevalid! He-he-he!" Ivan Ilyitch chuckled, attempting a jovial tone that felt slightly forced.

"And mumber, your Excellency," boomed the tall officer, seizing his chance to shine, "they say mumber instead of number!"

"Mumber! Oh yes, mumber instead of number!" Ivan Ilyitch echoed, managing another laugh. "To be sure, to be sure.... He-he-he!" The officer, visibly pleased, adjusted his tie with an air of accomplishment.

"And sometimes," interjected the young man from the satirical paper, his voice cutting through the brief lull, "nigh by instead of near."

Ivan Ilyitch, however, chose to ignore this. His chuckles, after all, were not for everyone.

"Nigh by," the young man persisted, his irritation evident. "Nigh by instead of near."

Ivan Ilyitch turned a stern gaze upon him, silencing him effectively. Pseldonimov, noticing the tension, leaned toward the young man and whispered, "Why insist? Let it go."

"But I was only talking. Mayn't one speak?" the young man grumbled under his breath, though he refrained from saying more and soon left the room. His exit was not to sulk but to retreat to the small back room, where refreshments awaited.

In the snug, dimly lit room, the young man poured himself a glass of vodka, his motions sharp with irritation. The medical student, the life of the dancing crowd with his disheveled hair and exuberance, bounded into the room, heading straight for the decanter.

"They're about to start again," the student exclaimed excitedly. "Come and see! I'm going to dance a solo on my head. After supper, I'll attempt the fish dance. It's perfect for a wedding—and a subtle jab at Pseldonimov too. Kleopatra Semyonovna—what a lively one she is! You can try anything with her!"

"He's a reactionary," the young man from the satirical paper muttered gloomily, tossing back his vodka.

"Who's a reactionary?" the student asked, already half out the door.

"That 'personage,' the one they're pampering with sweets. He's a reactionary, I tell you."

"What nonsense," the student dismissed with a wave, rushing back to the dance floor as the music struck up. Left alone, the young man on the satirical paper poured another drink. As the alcohol took hold, his irritation deepened into a simmering resentment against Ivan Ilyitch, who had slighted him so cruelly.

Meanwhile, in the main room, the atmosphere was shifting. Though Ivan Ilyitch had provided what he believed was a sufficient explanation for his presence, the guests had remained uneasy. Then, like magic, a whisper began to circulate: "He's a little ... under the influence." What had initially seemed a dreadful imposition now made perfect sense. The guests relaxed, their guarded politeness giving way to unrestrained merriment. Laughter rang out, voices grew louder, and the festivities resumed with renewed vigor.

The quadrille began. Just as Ivan Ilyitch prepared to address the bride with another carefully crafted remark, the tall officer dashed forward, dropped theatrically to one knee, and whisked her away before Ivan Ilyitch could protest. The bride, clearly relieved, didn't even glance back as she joined the dance.

"Well, she has every right to enjoy herself," Ivan Ilyitch mused, though inwardly he bristled. "And yet, it's evident—they simply don't know how to behave."

Turning to Pseldonimov, who hovered nearby with an almost canine devotion, he said, "Don't stand on ceremony, my dear Porfiry. Surely you have arrangements to attend to or something pressing.... Please, don't let me keep you."

Pseldonimov, with his perpetually bent neck and intent gaze, remained unmoving. His presence was becoming unbearable to Ivan Ilyitch, who thought with growing irritation, "Why is he watching me like that? What does he want?"

Akim Petrovitch, eager to play the dutiful host, seized a bottle of champagne and approached Ivan Ilyitch. "Will you allow me, your Excellency?" he asked, holding the bottle reverently, as though presenting a sacred offering.

"I ... I'm not sure I should...." Ivan Ilyitch began hesitantly.

But Akim Petrovitch, with an almost reverential glow, was already pouring. After filling Ivan Ilyitch's glass, he carefully poured a smaller amount for himself. His deference, bordering on obsequiousness, was both gratifying and irritating.

The general sipped his champagne—tepid and poor in quality—while Akim Petrovitch fidgeted beside him, clearly struggling to find a topic of conversation. Ivan Ilyitch, though frustrated, felt a small, fleeting satisfaction in the quiet acknowledgment of his authority.

Ivan Ilyitch glanced at the bottle and thought, "The old fellow probably wants a drink himself but doesn't dare take one until I do. I shouldn't stop him. Besides, it would look ridiculous to leave the bottle untouched between us." To break the silence, he took a sip, thinking it was better than just sitting there doing nothing.

"I'm here," he said slowly, pausing for emphasis between words, "I'm here, you might say, by chance. And naturally, there are some who might think it's ... inappropriate for someone like me to attend ... an event like this."

Akim Petrovitch, sitting nearby, didn't respond. He merely watched with timid curiosity.

"But I hope," Ivan Ilyitch continued, "you can understand why I've come. It's not just to drink wine ... he-he!" He let out a small laugh, attempting to lighten the mood.

Akim Petrovitch tried to join in with a chuckle of his own, imitating his superior, but the sound barely came out. He remained silent and offered no comforting reply.

"I'm here," Ivan Ilyitch went on, "to encourage you, to show, in a way, a moral purpose." He felt annoyed by Akim Petrovitch's lack of response, but before he could continue, he suddenly fell silent himself. He noticed that Akim Petrovitch had lowered his gaze as though he were guilty of some offense. Feeling slightly awkward, Ivan Ilyitch took another sip from his glass. At the same time, Akim Petrovitch hastily grabbed the bottle and refilled his superior's drink as if it were his only way to escape discomfort.

"You really don't have many ideas, do you?" Ivan Ilyitch thought, glaring at Akim Petrovitch, who, under the weight of that stern gaze, decided it was safer to remain silent and keep his eyes downcast. The two men sat side by side in an oppressive, awkward silence that lasted a couple of painful minutes.

A few words about Akim Petrovitch: he was a man of the old school, humble to the point of obsequiousness. From his earliest years, he had been trained to be meek and subservient, though he was a kind-hearted and honest man. He came from a family that had lived and worked in Petersburg for generations and had never set foot outside the city. This made him a very particular type of Russian, one whose entire world revolved around Petersburg, his workplace, and his modest salary. Russian traditions and songs were foreign to him, except perhaps "Lutchinushka," which he might have heard on a barrel organ.

Petersburg Russians could be recognized by two peculiar habits: first, they always referred to the local newspaper as the "Academic News" instead of the "Petersburg News." Second, they never said "breakfast," preferring the word "Frühstück," pronounced with a distinct emphasis on the first syllable. These traits made them stand out from other Russians. While Akim Petrovitch was no fool and could discuss his field of expertise intelligently, he thought it improper to respond to Ivan Ilyitch's lofty musings, though he was burning with curiosity about his superior's real motives.

Meanwhile, Ivan Ilyitch sank deeper into thought, sipping his drink absentmindedly every few moments. Akim Petrovitch dutifully refilled the glass each time. Both men sat in silence. Ivan Ilyitch's gaze wandered to the dancers, and something suddenly caught his attention.

The dancing was lively, full of unrestrained joy. The guests weren't particularly skilled dancers, but their sheer enthusiasm made up for it. The officer stood out, particularly in solos where he performed exaggerated moves, bending sharply to one side as though he might fall, only to recover with equal vigor in the opposite direction. He maintained a serious expression, fully convinced everyone was watching him.

Another guest, who had clearly had too much to drink, fell asleep beside his partner, leaving her to dance alone. A young clerk, meanwhile, repeatedly kissed the end of his partner's blue scarf as they crossed paths during the quadrille. His partner acted as though she didn't notice and glided along gracefully. The medical student even performed a headstand, earning wild applause and cheers from the crowd.

At first, Ivan Ilyitch found himself smiling at their uninhibited joy. He had hoped for this kind of carefree atmosphere, but as time passed, he began to feel uneasy. The revelry seemed almost disrespectful, as if the guests had forgotten his presence entirely. One woman, wearing a shabby second-hand velvet dress, even pinned her skirt to resemble trousers, to the delight of her dance partner.

"They were so reserved before, and now they're completely uninhibited," Ivan Ilyitch thought. "How did things change so quickly? Have they forgotten I'm here?"

Trying to recover his footing, Ivan Ilyitch turned to the medical student and said, "You dance remarkably well, young man." But deep down, he felt an unsettling doubt gnawing at him. Something had shifted, and he wasn't sure what.

The student suddenly turned toward Ivan Ilyitch, made a ridiculous face, and, leaning in so close that his breath could be felt, let out a loud, pitch-perfect imitation of a rooster's crow. It was so unexpected and absurd that the room erupted in raucous laughter. Despite his bewilderment, Ivan Ilyitch stood up, clutching his hat. The imitation was undeniably good, but the sheer brazenness of it was intolerable.

Just as Ivan Ilyitch was debating how to handle the situation, Pseldonimov appeared, bowing nervously, and invited him to join them for supper. His mother followed closely behind, adding her own earnest plea.

"Your Excellency," she said with a deep bow, "please, honor us. Don't disdain our humble offering."

"I… I'm not sure," Ivan Ilyitch stammered, still clutching his hat. "I didn't come here with that intention… I really should be going…."

At that very moment, he resolved internally to leave immediately, to escape the increasingly awkward situation. But somehow, despite his resolve, he found himself staying. A minute later, he was leading the group to the supper table. Pseldonimov and his mother cleared the way for him, treating him with exaggerated reverence, and seated him in the place of honor. A freshly opened bottle of champagne was placed beside his plate. Hors d'oeuvres—salt herring and vodka—were arranged before him.

Mechanically, Ivan Ilyitch reached for the vodka, poured himself a large glass, and downed it in one gulp. He had never drunk vodka before, and the sharp burn was overwhelming. He felt as though he were tumbling uncontrollably down a hill, unable to stop himself or grab hold of anything solid.

His situation had taken an undeniably bizarre turn. It felt as though fate itself were mocking him. How had things spiraled so far out of control in just an hour? He had entered the house with noble intentions, full of warmth and goodwill toward all humanity, eager to connect with his subordinates on a deeper level. Yet now, an hour later, he felt nothing but resentment. His heart ached with irritation toward Pseldonimov, his wife, and even the entire wedding itself.

Worse still, he could sense Pseldonimov's own disdain. The young clerk's expression seemed to say, "Why don't you leave already? Curse you for imposing yourself on us!" Ivan Ilyitch had read this silent plea in Pseldonimov's eyes for some time now.

Still, he could never have admitted—either to himself or aloud—that this interpretation might be accurate. His pride wouldn't allow it. Instead, he tried to convince himself that the night could still be salvaged. Yet, deep down, he felt suffocated and yearned for freedom, for air, for peace. He was too kind-hearted to cause a scene, too bound by the weight of social expectations to leave abruptly.

He chastised himself silently. "Why am I still here? Did I come to eat and drink?" As he tasted the herring, he felt a flicker of doubt, even skepticism, about the grand purpose of his visit. The lofty ideals that had driven him to enter the house now seemed faint and far away.

But leaving without a proper conclusion felt impossible. What would people think? Rumors would spread by morning—at the office, at social gatherings, at the homes of acquaintances like the Shembels and the Shubins. Stepan Nikiforovitch and Semyon Ivanovitch would undoubtedly hear of it. If he left now, he would seem like someone who frequented lowly company, someone who had lost his sense of decorum. No, he needed to find a way to make his moral purpose clear. He had to end the evening on a note of dignity.

Yet the right moment for such an exit refused to present itself. He felt increasingly alienated. "They don't even respect me," he thought bitterly. "What are they laughing at? They're so carefree, so lacking in decency. The younger generation is completely devoid of feeling!" Still, he resolved to stay. "Now that they're all gathered at the table, I'll seize the moment. I'll talk to them about serious matters—reforms, the greatness of Russia. I can still win them over. Perhaps it's not too late."

But his confidence wavered. "How should I begin? What approach should I take to capture their attention? I'm floundering here. They're laughing over there—are they laughing at me? Oh, heavens, what am I even doing here? Why don't I just leave? Why do I keep forcing myself to stay?"

These thoughts tormented him, and a deep, unbearable shame began to settle over him. He felt trapped, his dignity eroding with every passing moment. Yet despite his internal turmoil, the evening carried on, one awkward moment following another. It seemed there was no escape from this slow, painful unraveling of his intentions.

Within two minutes of sitting at the table, an alarming realization struck Ivan Ilyitch like a thunderbolt. He was dreadfully drunk—not just slightly intoxicated as he had been before, but completely and irredeemably so. The culprit was the glass of vodka he had consumed after the champagne, which had taken hold of him with alarming speed. Every fiber of his being was now overwhelmed by a creeping sense of weakness and instability. Though his confidence seemed to swell, a persistent, gnawing voice inside him cried out, "This is bad—terribly bad—and utterly inappropriate!"

His inebriated mind began to oscillate between two opposing states. On one side, he felt a swaggering self-assurance, a daring disregard for obstacles, and an almost reckless belief that he would achieve whatever goal he had in mind. But on the other side, a dull ache in his chest gnawed at him, whispering fears about the consequences. "What will they think? How will this end? What will happen tomorrow—tomorrow—tomorrow?" These thoughts tormented him.

Before, he had vaguely sensed that there might be enemies among the guests. Now, with a heart-sinking clarity, he became convinced of it. The signs were unmistakable, he thought. But why? What had he done to provoke such hostility? His bewilderment was as painful as his growing unease.

The table was crowded with thirty guests, many of whom had clearly had too much to drink. Some were behaving with unsettling boldness, shouting over one another, bawling out toasts out of turn, and even pelting the ladies with wads of bread. One particularly unkempt man, dressed in a greasy coat, had fallen off his chair the moment he sat down and remained sprawled on the floor for the entirety of supper. Another guest repeatedly attempted to stand on the table to deliver a toast, only to be restrained by the officer, who firmly grabbed his coat-tails and pulled him down each time.

The supper itself was chaotic, despite the supposed credentials of the hired cook, who had once worked for a general. The dishes included galantine, tongue with potatoes, rissoles with peas, a goose, and, finally, blancmange. As for drinks, there was beer, vodka, and sherry, though the only champagne was the bottle placed beside Ivan Ilyitch. This arrangement required him to pour for both himself and Akim Petrovitch, who lacked the nerve to help himself without explicit permission. The rest of the guests were left to make do with whatever alcohol they could find—be it Caucasian wine or something else.

The table itself was an awkward assembly of mismatched furniture, including a card table, all covered with an assortment of tablecloths, one of which was a brightly colored Yaroslav cloth. Guests were seated haphazardly, with men and women alternating in a disorganized manner. Pseldonimov's mother chose not to sit down, bustling around to supervise instead. However, another figure made her entrance during the meal—a woman in a faded reddish silk dress, wearing a high cap and a bandage around her face for toothache. This was the bride's mother, who had only emerged from a back room for supper, her appearance underscoring her hostility toward Pseldonimov's mother. This enmity would warrant further explanation later, but for now, her presence unsettled Ivan Ilyitch. She shot him spiteful, almost sarcastic glances and made no effort to be introduced to him. Her demeanor struck him as deeply suspicious.

But she wasn't the only one who put him on edge. As Ivan Ilyitch scanned the table, he found himself growing increasingly wary of several other guests. He couldn't shake the impression that some of them were conspiring against him. One man, a bearded artist of some kind, seemed especially ominous, frequently glancing at Ivan Ilyitch and whispering to the person beside him. Another guest, visibly drunk, nevertheless exuded a certain suspicious energy. The medical student, whose antics had already been questionable, now seemed to carry an undercurrent of unpredictability. Even the officer, though previously a source of mild annoyance, now struck Ivan Ilyitch as potentially unreliable.

The young man from the satirical paper, however, was the most aggravating presence at the table. Reclining insolently in his chair, he radiated arrogance and contempt. His loud snorting and smug expression were impossible to ignore. Although the other guests seemed to disregard him entirely—likely because his contributions to the literary world amounted to just four subpar poems published in The Firebrand—Ivan Ilyitch felt a burning irritation toward him. When a bread pellet landed suspiciously close to Ivan Ilyitch, he was convinced it had been hurled by none other than this insolent journalist.

question, about reform. They'll adore me, and I'll leave this gathering as a hero!"

These lofty dreams filled Ivan Ilyitch with a temporary warmth, but soon a less pleasant realization crept in. Something strange and undignified was happening to him—he was drooling. Saliva escaped his mouth uncontrollably, and he caught himself spitting unintentionally. Worse still, he noticed that a spray of spit had landed on Akim Petrovitch's cheek. Poor Akim Petrovitch, too polite to wipe it away, sat rigidly in discomfort. Embarrassed, Ivan Ilyitch hastily took a napkin and wiped it himself, but this action struck him as so absurd and inappropriate that he froze in mortification.

As he looked at Akim Petrovitch, Ivan Ilyitch realized something else: for the past fifteen minutes, he had been speaking animatedly about some important subject, yet Akim Petrovitch seemed more nervous and frightened than engaged. Pseldonimov, sitting just one chair away, leaned in with a peculiar, almost watchful air, his head tilted slightly to one side as though scrutinizing Ivan Ilyitch. It was as if he were waiting for something specific, something unsettling. Glancing around the room, Ivan Ilyitch noticed that several guests were openly staring at him, and some were even laughing. Yet, oddly enough, he didn't feel embarrassed—in fact, he doubled down.

Taking another sip from his glass, he suddenly raised his voice to ensure everyone could hear him. "I was just saying," he began, loudly and deliberately, "I was just saying to Akim Petrovitch here, ladies and gentlemen, that Russia... yes, Russia... in my view, is currently experiencing a significant period of hu-hu-manity."

From the far end of the table came a mocking echo: "Hu-hu-manity!"

"Hu-hu!"

"Tu-tu!"

Ivan Ilyitch stopped mid-sentence, startled. Pseldonimov stood abruptly, craning his neck to locate the source of the interruptions, while Akim Petrovitch subtly shook his head, as though scolding the unruly guests. Ivan Ilyitch saw the gesture but was too flustered to respond. Instead, he resumed, his voice firmer but tinged with desperation: "Humanity! Yes, that is what I meant! And just this evening, I was telling Stepan Niki-ki-foro-vitch... yes, I told him... that we are on the brink of a great regeneration, so to speak, of everything..."

But his words began to trail off as his confidence wavered. He couldn't shake the sensation that the room, once so full of possibility, now felt unwelcoming, even hostile. Still, he pressed on, as though sheer determination might salvage his dignity.

"Your Excellency!" came a loud exclamation from the far end of the table.

"What is it you want?" Ivan Ilyitch asked, halting his speech and trying to identify the speaker.

"Nothing at all, your Excellency. I got carried away. Please, continue! Continue!" the voice called out again.

Ivan Ilyitch felt a pang of irritation. "The regeneration, so to speak, of those same things..." he began again, only to be interrupted once more.

"Your Excellency!" the voice shouted louder.

"What now?"

"How do you do!"

Ivan Ilyitch could no longer suppress his frustration. He broke off entirely and turned toward the source of the disruption. It was a very young man, still a schoolboy, who was evidently quite drunk and had already drawn suspicion. This boy had been causing disturbances throughout the evening, breaking glasses and plates in his misguided belief that such antics were appropriate for a wedding. At the very moment Ivan Ilyitch fixed his gaze on him, the officer at the table had already begun reprimanding the unruly lad.

"What do you think you're doing? Why are you yelling? If you don't behave, we'll throw you out!" the officer barked.

"I didn't mean you, Your Excellency! I didn't mean you. Please, continue!" the drunken schoolboy slurred, slouching in his chair. "I'm listening. I'm ve-ry, ve-ry, ve-ry much enjoying it! Praiseworthy, praiseworthy!"

"The boy is drunk," Pseldonimov whispered anxiously to Ivan Ilyitch.

"I can see that, but..."

"I was just telling a very amusing story, Your Excellency!" the officer interjected, trying to redirect attention. "It's about a lieutenant in our company who used to behave just like that with his superiors, always saying 'praiseworthy, praiseworthy' to everything. He ended up being dismissed from the army ten years ago."

"What kind of lieutenant was that?" Ivan Ilyitch asked, attempting to reestablish some order.

"He was in our company, Your Excellency. The poor man went completely mad over the word 'praiseworthy.' At first, they tried gentle methods to address it, but eventually, he was put under arrest. His commanding officer even tried to counsel him like a father, but he just kept repeating, 'praiseworthy, praiseworthy.' Strangely enough, he was a tall, imposing man—over six feet! They were considering a court-martial when they realized he was genuinely insane."

"So... a schoolboy's antics should not be taken too seriously," Ivan Ilyitch said, attempting to smooth things over. "For my part, I am prepared to overlook this."

"They conducted a medical inquiry into the lieutenant's condition, Your Excellency," the officer continued.

"Good heavens, but the man was alive, wasn't he?" Ivan Ilyitch asked, perplexed.

"What? Did they dissect him?" someone quipped loudly, triggering a wave of laughter from the guests.

The laughter grew louder and more raucous. It spread across the table, infecting nearly everyone present, many of whom had otherwise behaved with restraint until that moment. Ivan Ilyitch felt a hot flush of anger and humiliation rise within him.

"Ladies and gentlemen!" he shouted, struggling to maintain his composure but stumbling over his words, "I am perfectly capable of comprehending that a man is not dissected while alive. What I meant to say was... I assumed he had died as a result of his condition... or that he ceased to exist in some way... I mean to say that you don't like me, but I... I like all of you... yes, even

Por... Porfiry! And yet, here I am, lowering myself to explain myself to you!"

At that moment, Ivan Ilyitch unintentionally spat on the tablecloth in the middle of his impassioned outburst. A large, conspicuous spot of saliva landed directly in front of him. Pseldonimov leapt forward, snatching up a napkin to wipe it clean, but the incident only deepened Ivan Ilyitch's despair.

"My friends, this is too much!" he cried out in frustration.

"The man is drunk, Your Excellency," Pseldonimov whispered again, visibly trembling.

"Porfiry, I see what's happening here... yes, I see it. But I must ask you all, in what way have I lowered myself?" Ivan Ilyitch implored, his voice cracking with emotion.

His plea was met with a chilling silence. It was a silence so absolute, so damning, that it crushed Ivan Ilyitch's last shred of hope. "At least someone could shout something at this moment!" he thought bitterly. But the guests exchanged only awkward glances, leaving him adrift. Akim Petrovitch sat frozen, as though petrified, while Pseldonimov's pale, stricken face betrayed a single haunting thought: What will this cost me tomorrow?

At last, breaking the unbearable tension, the young man from the satirical paper—now thoroughly drunk but seething with pent-up animosity—spoke up with piercing clarity.

"Yes," he said, his voice loud and accusatory. "Yes, you have lowered yourself. You're a reactionary... a re-ac-tion-ary!"

"Young man, mind your manners! To whom do you think you're speaking?" Ivan Ilyitch roared, springing to his feet in indignation.

"To you! And I am not a young man!" the journalist retorted, his eyes blazing. "You came here to show off, to pretend at being humane, and to win applause. But all you've done is ruin the evening for everyone. You've been guzzling champagne without a second thought, knowing it's far beyond the means of a clerk who earns ten roubles a month. And let's not overlook the fact that you high-ranking officials are often far too fond of the young wives of your subordinates. Yes, I said it! And I'll add this: you support state monopolies!"

Pandemonium erupted. Ivan Ilyitch turned to Pseldonimov, his face a mixture of fury and disbelief. "Pseldonimov, what does this mean?" he demanded.

But Pseldonimov stood paralyzed, his face drained of all color, utterly incapable of offering an explanation. The other guests remained in stunned silence, save for the artist and the schoolboy, who clapped and shouted, "Bravo, bravo!" The young journalist, emboldened by the chaos, continued his tirade with unrestrained venom. Ivan Ilyitch, shaken to his core, realized he had lost all control of the situation.

"Pseldonimov! Pseldonimov!" Ivan Ilyitch called out desperately, reaching his hands toward him. Every word from the sarcastic young man felt like a sharp dagger piercing his heart, twisting deeper with each phrase.

"Right away, Your Excellency! Please, don't trouble yourself!" Pseldonimov responded quickly, darting toward the offending young man. He grabbed him firmly by the collar and yanked him away from the table. It was surprising to see such strength from someone as frail-looking as Pseldonimov, but the young man, being heavily drunk, was in no condition to resist. Pseldonimov landed a few firm slaps on the man's back and shoved him out through the door.

"You're all a bunch of scoundrels!" the young man shouted as he stumbled out. "I'll draw caricatures of every one of you in The Firebrand tomorrow!"

The remaining guests jumped from their seats in shock.

"Your Excellency! Please, don't be upset!" Pseldonimov's mother, along with several others, hurried over to calm Ivan Ilyitch. "Everything is fine, Your Excellency!" they pleaded.

"No, no!" Ivan Ilyitch cried out, his voice trembling with anguish. "I am destroyed! I came here with nothing but good intentions. I wanted to bless you, to give you my best wishes, and this—this is the thanks I get? For everything I've done?"

He collapsed into a chair as if his strength had completely left him. Resting both arms on the table, he buried his face in them, right into a plate of blancmange. A wave of horror rippled through the room, leaving everyone frozen in stunned silence.

Moments later, Ivan Ilyitch stirred, seemingly trying to get up. He wavered unsteadily, then staggered forward, tripping over a chair leg. With a heavy thud, he fell flat onto the floor. Almost immediately, a loud snore escaped from him.

This is often what happens to those unaccustomed to alcohol when they overindulge. They remain conscious until the very last moment, only to collapse as if struck down. Ivan Ilyitch now lay on the floor, completely unconscious. Pseldonimov stood over him, clutching at his hair in utter despair, frozen as if he had turned to stone.

Meanwhile, the guests began leaving hurriedly, each offering their own whispered remarks about the night's dramatic turn of events as they departed. By then, it was close to three in the morning.

Yet, as chaotic as the scene was, Pseldonimov's situation was far graver than it appeared at first glance. His circumstances were much worse than anyone could imagine, given the already dismal surroundings. While Ivan Ilyitch lay unconscious on the floor and Pseldonimov wrestled with his growing panic, we must pause the story for a moment to provide some background on the life of Porfiry Petrovitch Pseldonimov.

Less than a month before his wedding, Pseldonimov had been living in desperate poverty. He came from a provincial town where his father had worked in some government office but died while awaiting trial for unspecified charges. Five months before the wedding, Pseldonimov had been enduring terrible hardship in Petersburg for a year. When he finally secured a position paying ten roubles a month, it briefly lifted his spirits and improved his health. However, this small improvement did not last, and harsh circumstances soon crushed him again.

The only family he had left in the world was his mother, who had moved to Petersburg with him after his father's death. Together, they lived in freezing conditions and survived on the most meager and questionable food. There were days when Pseldonimov himself walked to the Fontanka River with a jug to fetch drinking water. When he finally got his job, he managed to rent a small corner of a room for himself and his mother. She began taking in laundry to help make ends meet, while he saved every penny over four months to buy himself a pair of boots and an overcoat.

At work, he faced endless difficulties. His superiors openly ridiculed him, asking, "When was the last time you had a bath?" Rumors circulated that his uniform collar harbored nests of bugs. Despite this, Pseldonimov was a man of remarkable inner strength. Outwardly, he was mild and unassuming, with only the barest hint of education, and he rarely spoke about anything. Whether he had dreams, plans, or deep thoughts remained uncertain, but within him grew an unshakable, instinctive resolve to escape his miserable circumstances. He was persistent, like an ant that rebuilds its nest no matter how many times it is destroyed. Pseldonimov was determined to carve out a better life, build his own home, and perhaps even save money for the future.

His mother was the one person who loved him unconditionally, and her love was unwavering. She was a hardworking and tireless woman, full of resolve yet kindhearted. Together, they might have managed to scrape by in their tiny corner for five or six years, waiting for their luck to change. But their lives took a different turn when they crossed paths with a retired titular councillor named Mlekopitaev.

Mlekopitaev had once been a clerk in the treasury and served in the provinces but had since settled in Petersburg with his family. He had known Pseldonimov's father and owed him a favor. Although Mlekopitaev had some money, no one—not even his wife, eldest daughter, or relatives—knew exactly how much he possessed. He had two daughters and was known for being a cruel bully, a heavy drinker, and a domestic tyrant. Adding to this, he was also an invalid, confined to a chair due to a disease that didn't stop him from drinking vodka.

Mlekopitaev spent his days drinking and swearing, finding amusement in tormenting those around him. His household was a collection of relatives he could endlessly bully. Among them were his sickly sister, two of his wife's ill-natured sisters, an elderly aunt with a broken rib, and even a German woman who entertained him with stories from The Arabian Nights. These women, along with his long-suffering wife—who had suffered from chronic toothache since birth—were all subjected to his relentless verbal abuse. He delighted in stirring up quarrels among them, encouraging spiteful gossip and discord, only to laugh at their misery.

His joy reached new heights when his widowed eldest daughter, along with her three sickly children, moved in after years of living in poverty with her late husband. Though he hated her children, he relished the opportunity to use them as more fodder for his cruel amusement. All of these unfortunate women and children, along with their tormentor, were crammed into a small wooden house on the Petersburg Side. They were constantly hungry because Mlekopitaev was miserly, doling out money in tiny amounts, although he spared no expense on vodka for himself. They also suffered from lack of sleep, as the old man's insomnia demanded constant entertainment.

Amid this chaos, Mlekopitaev noticed Pseldonimov. Something about his long nose and submissive demeanor appealed to him. His younger daughter, weak and unattractive, had just turned seventeen. Though she had attended a German school, she had learned little more than the alphabet. She grew up sickly, anemic, and perpetually terrified of her drunken, crippled father. Her home life was a toxic environment of bickering, eavesdropping, and constant scolding. With no friends and limited intelligence, she had long been eager to marry. While she remained silent in public, at home, she was spiteful and quarrelsome, often pinching and scolding her sister's children. This behavior led to constant fights with her elder sister.

One day, Mlekopitaev decided to offer this younger daughter to Pseldonimov as a bride. Despite Pseldonimov's miserable state, he hesitated, asking for time to think it over. Both he and his mother were torn. The young woman's dowry included a house—small, wooden, and unimpressive, but still a property—and four hundred roubles, a sum it would take Pseldonimov years to save on his own.

Mlekopitaev, drunk and domineering, declared his intentions loudly. "What am I taking this man into my house for?" he bellowed. "First, because I'm surrounded by women, and I'm sick of it! I want Pseldonimov to dance to my tune because I'm his benefactor. And second, I'll do it to spite all of you since you don't want it to happen. I've made my decision! And you, Porfiry, you'll beat her when she's your wife. She's had seven devils in her since the day she was born. Beat them out of her, and I'll have the stick ready for you."

Pseldonimov said nothing, but he had already made up his mind. Before the wedding, both he and his mother were brought into the household, cleaned up, given proper clothes, boots, and even some money for the upcoming celebration. The old man took them under his wing, perhaps precisely because the rest of the family disliked them. Oddly enough, he seemed to genuinely like Pseldonimov's mother, so much so that he refrained from mocking her. However, his attitude toward Pseldonimov was different. A week before the wedding, he made Pseldonimov perform a Cossack dance in front of him.

"That's enough," he said when the dance ended. "I just wanted to see if you still remembered your place with me."

He allowed just enough money to cover the cost of the wedding, with not a single kopek to spare. He invited all his relatives and acquaintances, ensuring a full house. On Pseldonimov's side, however, the only attendees were the young man who wrote for The Firebrand and Akim Petrovitch, who was considered the guest of honor. Pseldonimov was painfully aware that his bride disliked him and had desperately hoped to marry the officer instead. Still, he endured it all because he had made a pact with his mother to go through with it.

The wedding day was a nightmare. The old man spent the entire day drunk, shouting insults, and using foul language. The rest of the family fled to the back rooms, cramming together in suffocating quarters, while the front rooms were reserved for dancing and supper. At last, the old man passed out, completely drunk, at around eleven o'clock. It was then that the bride's mother, who had been especially displeased with

Pseldonimov's mother that day, decided to bury her grudge, adopt a gracious demeanor, and join the gathering. But everything turned upside down with Ivan Ilyitch's unexpected arrival.

Madame Mlekopitaev, overwhelmed with embarrassment, began complaining that she hadn't been informed about the general's attendance. She was assured that he had come uninvited, but her stubborn nature refused to believe it. Champagne had to be found immediately. Pseldonimov's mother only had one rouble, while Pseldonimov himself didn't even have a single kopek. He was forced to beg his ill-tempered mother-in-law for the money to buy not just one bottle but two. They pleaded with her, citing his future career prospects and the need to maintain appearances for the sake of his professional life. After much persuasion, she finally gave them the money, but not without subjecting Pseldonimov to a torrent of bitter insults. The humiliation was so overwhelming that, several times, he ran into the room where the bridal bed had been prepared. There, shaking with anger and frustration, he buried his head in the bedding meant for his wedding night, unable to contain his despair.

Ivan Ilyitch, of course, had no idea about the price Pseldonimov had paid—both financially and emotionally—for the two bottles of Jackson champagne he had consumed that evening. And when the general's visit ended in such an unfortunate way, Pseldonimov's horror and misery only deepened. He faced the prospect of endless complaints and recriminations from his peevish new bride and her unreasonable relatives. His head was already pounding, his vision blurred, and he felt dizzy with exhaustion. On top of that, Ivan Ilyitch now needed someone to take care of him. At three o'clock in the morning, Pseldonimov had to find a doctor or a carriage to take him home. And not just any carriage—it had to be a proper one, as letting an ordinary cabman drive him in his condition was unthinkable. But where could Pseldonimov find the money for even that?

Madame Mlekopitaev, still furious that the general hadn't said a single word to her or even acknowledged her presence at supper, declared she didn't have a single kopek. Perhaps she truly didn't. But that left Pseldonimov at a complete loss. Where could he get the money? What could he possibly do? No wonder he felt like tearing his hair out in frustration.

Meanwhile, Ivan Ilyitch was moved to a small leather sofa in the dining room while the tables were cleared away. Pseldonimov ran frantically from one person to another, desperately trying to borrow money. He even asked the servants, but none of them had anything to spare. In his desperation, he approached Akim Petrovitch, who had lingered after the other guests had left. But although Akim Petrovitch was kind-hearted, the mere mention of money seemed to alarm him. He stammered, his face filled with confusion and embarrassment.

"Another time, with pleasure," he muttered, "but now ... you must really excuse me...."

Taking his cap, Pseldonimov ran out of the house as quickly as he could. Only the kind young man who had talked about the dream book stayed behind to help, though even his assistance didn't lead to much. He sincerely sympathized with Pseldonimov's troubles and stayed to offer his support. After much discussion, Pseldonimov, his mother, and the young man decided not to call a doctor. Instead, they agreed to get a carriage to take the sick man home and to use home remedies in the meantime. They applied cold water to his head and temples, placed ice on his forehead, and tried other similar measures while waiting for the carriage. Pseldonimov's mother took charge of these tasks, while the young man dashed out in search of a carriage.

Finding transportation at that hour on the Petersburg Side proved difficult. The young man had to go to distant livery stables, wake up the coachmen, and begin bargaining. They initially demanded five roubles, claiming it was reasonable for the time of night. Finally, they agreed to come for three roubles. However, by the time the carriage arrived—just before five o'clock—the plan had changed. Ivan Ilyitch's condition had worsened. He was still unconscious, moaning and tossing so violently that moving him had become dangerous and unsafe.

"What's next?" Pseldonimov exclaimed in utter despair. The new problem was where to put the ailing man if he stayed in the house. There were only two proper beds: a large double bed where old Mlekopitaev and his wife slept and a newly purchased walnut bed meant for the newlyweds. Everyone else in the house slept on makeshift feather beds laid out on the floor, most of which were in poor condition and unsuitable for a guest of Ivan Ilyitch's status. Even these were insufficient, and there wasn't a single extra one available.

The most suitable spot seemed to be the drawing room, as it was farthest from the family's living quarters and had a door leading to the passage. But how could they make up a proper bed in there? Certainly not on chairs—that was only suitable for schoolboys visiting home for a weekend, and it would be deeply disrespectful to put someone like Ivan Ilyitch on such an arrangement. The only remaining option was the bridal bed.

This bed was in a small room adjoining the dining room. It was furnished with a brand-new double mattress, pristine sheets, and four pillows covered in frilled muslin cases. The satin quilt was pink and beautifully quilted with patterns, and muslin curtains hung from a golden ring above the bed. Everything had been carefully arranged, and the guests had admired the charming decor. Although the bride harbored a strong dislike for Pseldonimov, she had sneaked in several times during the evening to admire the room. When she learned that Ivan Ilyitch—suffering from what seemed to be mild cholera—was to be placed on her bridal bed, her indignation and fury were boundless.

Her mother sided with her, launching into a tirade and threatening to complain to her husband the next day. But Pseldonimov stood firm and insisted. Ivan Ilyitch was moved to the bridal chamber, and the newlyweds had to make do with a bed improvised from chairs. The bride whimpered and felt like pinching her husband in frustration but dared not disobey. She knew her father's temper too well—his crutch was a constant reminder of his authority—and feared the consequences of defying Pseldonimov. As a small consolation, the pink satin quilt and the decorative pillows were taken to the drawing room.

At that moment, the young man returned with the carriage, only to find it was no longer needed. Horrified, he realized he would have to pay for it himself, even though he didn't have a single coin to his name.

Pseldonimov, explaining he was completely broke, tried to reason with the driver. The driver, however, grew noisy and began pounding on the shutters. The situation escalated, and in the end, the young man was taken as a sort of hostage to Peski. He hoped to wake a student friend staying on Fourth Rozhdensky Street and borrow some money from him.

By six in the morning, the newlyweds were finally left alone in the drawing room. Pseldonimov's mother, however, spent the entire night by Ivan Ilyitch's side. She lay on a rug on the floor, covered with an old coat, and couldn't sleep because she had to tend to him constantly. Ivan Ilyitch suffered from severe colic, and Madame Pseldonimov—a woman of remarkable courage and dedication—personally undressed him, took care of his needs as if he were her own child, and tirelessly carried basins across the passage all night long. Yet, even with all this, the disasters of that fateful night were far from over.

Just ten minutes after the young couple had been left alone in the drawing room, a piercing scream echoed through the house. It wasn't a joyful cry but a sharp, alarming shriek that sent chills through the air. The scream was quickly followed by a crash, the sound of chairs collapsing, and the unmistakable clamor of chaos. A flood of shouting, frightened women, dressed in all sorts of disheveled nightwear, burst into the dark room. Among them were the bride's mother, her elder sister who had momentarily abandoned her sick children, and three aunts—one of whom, despite her broken rib, had managed to join the commotion. Even the cook and the German storyteller, whose prized feather bed had been confiscated for the young couple's use, trailed in with the others.

These women, driven by insatiable curiosity, had tiptoed out of the kitchen a quarter of an hour earlier and had been eavesdropping in the anteroom. When someone lit a candle, the scene that greeted them was shocking. The chairs that had supported the edges of the feather bed had given way, causing the bed to collapse onto the floor. The bride was sobbing in frustration, deeply offended by the incident. Pseldonimov stood there like a criminal caught red-handed, too humiliated to defend himself. Cries and accusations erupted from all sides. Pseldonimov's mother rushed in at the sound of the commotion, but the bride's mother immediately took control of the situation. She unleashed a storm of accusations, many of them exaggerated or entirely undeserved, saying things like, "What kind of husband are you after this? What good are you now after such a disgrace?"

Eventually, she took her daughter away, declaring she would take full responsibility when her fearsome husband demanded an explanation. The other women followed, shaking their heads and voicing their disapproval. Left alone, Pseldonimov's mother tried to console her son, but he quickly sent her away. He was beyond comfort.

Pseldonimov sank onto the sofa, barefoot and still in his nightclothes, utterly overwhelmed. His thoughts spiraled in all directions. Occasionally, his eyes wandered around the room, which not long ago had been filled with dancing and celebration. Now, the lingering smoke of cigarettes, scattered sweet wrappers, and the wreckage of the bridal bed told a grim story of how quickly joyful dreams could turn to dust. He sat there for nearly an hour, consumed by oppressive thoughts. One particularly painful realization was that he would have to transfer to a different office. There was no way he could stay where he was after everything that had happened. He also dreaded what Mlekopitaev might do, imagining the old man forcing him to dance the Cossack dance again to prove his obedience.

He thought bitterly about the fifty roubles Mlekopitaev had contributed to the wedding, all of which had been spent, and the fact that no one had mentioned the promised four hundred roubles—or even formally transferring the house to him. His thoughts wandered to his new wife, who had abandoned him at such a critical moment, and to the tall officer who had knelt before her during the wedding festivities. He recalled the seven devils her father claimed she had and the crutch supposedly ready to drive them out. Although Pseldonimov believed himself capable of enduring much, the unrelenting barrage of hardships made him doubt his resilience.

As these thoughts tormented him, the flickering candle cast his distorted shadow on the wall. His elongated neck, hooked nose, and tufts of hair created a surreal and haunting image. At last, chilled by the early morning air, he dragged himself to the collapsed feather bed. Without fixing anything or even extinguishing the dying candle, he lay down, too drained to care, and fell into a deep, almost lifeless sleep, the kind of sleep a man might have before facing a flogging.

Meanwhile, Ivan Ilyitch Pralinsky was enduring his own private torment on the now-desecrated bridal bed. His suffering was relentless—headaches, nausea, and a string of other unbearable symptoms kept him in constant agony. When fleeting moments of clarity did come, they brought visions so dreadful that unconsciousness seemed preferable. His mind was a jumbled mess. He vaguely recognized Pseldonimov's mother, who tended to him with gentle reassurances like, "Be patient, dear sir. It will pass soon." Although he recognized her, he couldn't make sense of her presence. Grotesque images haunted him, including visions of Semyon Ivanitch, who, upon closer inspection, seemed to morph into Pseldonimov's nose.

Other unsettling figures appeared in his fevered mind: the flamboyant artist, the officer, and the old woman with her face wrapped in cloth. Strangely, he found himself fixated on the golden ring from which the curtains above the bed hung. In the dim candlelight, it seemed to glow, and he became obsessed with its purpose. He asked the old woman about it several times but couldn't make himself understood, nor could she grasp what he wanted to know. Finally, by morning, the worst of his symptoms subsided, and he slipped into a deep, dreamless sleep.

When he awoke an hour later, his headache was excruciating, and his mouth felt unbearably dry and foul. As he sat up, the pale morning light streamed through the cracks in the shutters, casting a thin beam on the wall. It was seven o'clock. With horrifying clarity, he recalled the events of the previous night—his failed speech, his grand gesture gone awry, and the utter humiliation that awaited him in the eyes of others. Looking around the room, he saw the chaotic state of the bridal chamber and realized how thoroughly he had ruined it. Overwhelmed with shame and despair, he let out a cry, buried his face in his hands, and collapsed back onto the pillow.

A minute later, he jumped out of bed and noticed his clothes neatly folded and brushed on a chair. In a frenzy, he began dressing as quickly as he could, throwing panicked glances around the room as if expecting something dreadful to happen. On another chair nearby lay his greatcoat, fur cap, and yellow gloves. Intent on sneaking away unnoticed, he reached for his belongings. Just then, the door opened, and Pseldonimov's mother walked in, carrying an earthenware jug and basin. With a towel slung over her shoulder, she set the jug down and, without saying much, firmly informed him that he needed to wash.

"Come on, dear sir, wash yourself; you can't leave without freshening up," said the old woman.

At that moment, Ivan Ilyitch realized that if there was anyone in the world he didn't need to fear or feel embarrassed around, it was this old lady. He complied and washed. Later in his life, during moments of deep regret, he often recalled this scene vividly—the earthenware basin, the porcelain jug filled with icy water that still had floating ice chunks, and the oval soap wrapped in pink paper embossed with letters, clearly bought for the newlyweds but used by him instead. He remembered the old lady standing there with a linen towel draped over her shoulder. The cold water revived him, and after drying his face, he grabbed his hat, flung on the coat Pseldonimov handed him, and dashed across the hallway and through the kitchen. The cat was meowing, and the cook, still sitting on her bed, watched him leave with wide, curious eyes. Ivan Ilyitch hurried outside to the yard and then into the street, where he jumped into the first sledge he could find.

The morning was frosty, wrapped in a yellowish fog that blurred the surroundings. He turned up his coat collar, convinced that everyone he passed was staring at him, recognizing him.

For eight days, he stayed home, avoiding both the office and the outside world. He was ill, though more from emotional distress than physical sickness. Those days were like living in a personal hell, and he often thought they might count against him in the afterlife. At times, he even considered becoming a monk and retreating to a monastery. His imagination wandered during those days, conjuring images of mournful chanting, open coffins, solitary cells, dense forests, and dark caves. But when he snapped back to reality, he quickly dismissed these thoughts as absurd and felt ashamed of himself for entertaining such fantasies.

Then came waves of moral torment about his failed life. Shame would engulf him, burning through his soul like fire and reopening his inner wounds. He cringed at the thought of what people might say about him, how they would react when he returned to the office. He pictured whispers trailing him for years, perhaps even his whole life. His story, he feared, would become infamous. At times, he sank into such despair that he imagined going to Semyon Ivanovitch to ask for forgiveness and friendship. He didn't even try to justify his actions; instead, he blamed himself entirely, finding no excuse or defense for what had happened.

He also thought about resigning from his position and dedicating himself to living humbly, contributing to humanity as an ordinary citizen. At the very least, he considered cutting ties with everyone he knew, erasing all memory of himself. But this plan, too, felt unrealistic. Then he wondered if adopting a stricter demeanor at work might restore order and respect. This gave him moments of renewed hope and determination. Finally, after eight days of inner turmoil, he decided he couldn't bear the uncertainty any longer and resolved to return to the office.

For days, he had rehearsed this moment in his mind, imagining every detail of his return. He was certain he would be met with whispers, knowing glances, and smirks. Yet to his astonishment, none of that happened. His colleagues greeted him with respect, bowing politely and maintaining a professional demeanor. Everyone seemed busy with their work, and no one acted out of the ordinary. His heart filled with relief as he walked to his office.

He immediately threw himself into his tasks with seriousness. He reviewed reports, answered questions, and resolved issues with a sharpness and clarity he hadn't felt in a long time. He noticed that his colleagues seemed satisfied with his decisions and treated him with the same respect as always. Even the most sensitive observer wouldn't have found a trace of mockery or disrespect.

Eventually, Akim Petrovitch entered with some paperwork. Seeing him gave Ivan Ilyitch a brief pang of unease, but he quickly recovered. They discussed the matter at hand, and Ivan Ilyitch explained things with his usual authority. The only thing he noticed was that Akim Petrovitch avoided meeting his eyes, and Ivan Ilyitch found himself doing the same. When they finished, Akim Petrovitch began gathering his papers.

"There's one more thing," Akim Petrovitch said in a dry tone. "The clerk Pseldonimov has submitted a request to transfer to another department. His Excellency Semyon Ivanovitch Shipulenko has offered him a position. He asks for your approval."

"Oh, so he's transferring," Ivan Ilyitch replied, feeling as though a heavy burden had been lifted from his chest. He glanced at Akim Petrovitch, and for a moment, their eyes met. "Of course, I have no objection. I approve," he said.

Akim Petrovitch appeared eager to leave as quickly as possible. But in a surge of emotion, Ivan Ilyitch decided to speak further. Inspiration seemed to strike him.

"Tell him," Ivan Ilyitch began, fixing Akim Petrovitch with a look of sincerity, "tell Pseldonimov that I hold no grudge. None at all! On the contrary, I am willing to forget everything that happened, completely forget it…"

But Ivan Ilyitch stopped mid-sentence, startled by Akim Petrovitch's odd reaction. Instead of listening attentively, Akim Petrovitch blushed deeply, made hurried little bows, and edged toward the door as if desperate to escape. His awkward behavior made him seem almost foolish, as though he couldn't wait to get back to his desk.

Left alone, Ivan Ilyitch rose from his chair, feeling unsettled. He glanced at himself in the mirror without really noticing his reflection.

"No, strictness—strictness and nothing else," he muttered under his breath. But suddenly, his face flushed deeply, and a fresh wave of shame overwhelmed him. The weight of it felt even heavier than during his most agonizing days at home. "I broke down," he thought bitterly and sank back into his chair, utterly defeated.

Thank you for Reading

You've Just Read a Piece of the Greatest Library Ever Rebuilt

Thank you for reading.

This book is one of thousands we're restoring, reimagining, and translating as part of the **Modern Library of Alexandria** — a global movement to preserve and share humanity's most important ideas.

What was once lost to fire and time is now rising again — not just as memory, but as living, breathing knowledge, freely accessible to all.

What You Can Do Next:

- **Keep Reading.**

  Discover more legendary works — in beautiful print, audiobook, or digital form — at LibraryofAlexandria.com.

- **Build Your Own Library.**

  Every title is available as a paperback, hardcover, or collectible boxset — at true printing cost. Craft a personal library worthy of display.

- **Spread the Light.**

  Share this book. Tell others about the movement. Help us translate every timeless work into every language, so no reader is ever left behind.

By finishing this book, you've already taken part in something extraordinary.

Join us at LibraryofAlexandria.com

Together, we're rebuilding the greatest library the world has ever known.

With appreciation,
The Modern Library of Alexandria Team

Visit:

www.libraryofalexandria.com

Or scan the code below: